SIMON MANN:
THE REAL STORY

SIMON MANN:
THE REAL STORY

Sue Blackhall

Pen & Sword
MILITARY

First published in Great Britain in 2011 by
Pen & Sword Military
an imprint of
Pen & Sword Books Ltd
47 Church Street
Barnsley
South Yorkshire
S70 2AS

ISBN: 978-1-84884-577-0

Typeset in 11/13pt Palatino by
Concept, Huddersfield, West Yorkshire

Printed and bound in England by
the MPG Books Group

Pen & Sword Books Ltd incorporates the Imprints of Pen & Sword
Aviation, Pen & Sword Family History, Pen & Sword Maritime, Pen &
Sword Military, Pen & Sword Discovery, Wharncliffe Local History,
Wharncliffe True Crime, Wharncliffe Transport, Pen & Sword Select, Pen
& Sword Military Classics, Leo Cooper, The Praetorian Press, Remember
When, Seaforth Publishing and Frontline Publishing.

For a complete list of Pen & Sword titles please contact
PEN & SWORD BOOKS LIMITED
47 Church Street, Barnsley, South Yorkshire, S70 2AS, England
E-mail: enquiries@pen-and-sword.co.uk
Website: www.pen-and-sword.co.uk

Contents

Introduction

It had all the ingredients of a best-selling thriller – the clandestine activities of mercenaries; an impossibly daredevil plot to topple the regime of one of the world's most corrupt countries; the 'boy's own' approach by arrogant old public school pupils; and the controversy and intrigue from within governmental departments. Add in high-profile figures embroiled in the plot and the far-reaching repercussions and you have what was to become one of the most talked-about exploits of the twenty-first century.

In retrospect, the attempted coup on the tiny African country of Equatorial Guinea was always destined to fail. Even the coup's leader, Simon Mann, was forced to admit it. For it was a plot of such daring and involving so many, that it was guaranteed to attract attention before it even got off the ground; whispered talks amongst its perpetrators became shouted words of warning to those who monitored the meetings. The gathering of nearly 70 men just had to include those whose loyalty to the mission was questionable.

Would it really be possible to rid Equatorial Guinea of its brutal and corrupt leader and replace him with an exile from Spain? And to assume that the task in hand would be accomplished without challenge? Such secrets are hard to keep when there are over-ambitious hands reaching out to achieve it – and to grasp the high rewards. The characters involved already had a mystique about them they would wish to remain as such. They have lived lives on the edge in the eyes of the law and in the eyes of global spectators. Their intentions have often been dubious; their professional challenges dangerous.

It is because of the country's dark infamy that I felt the need to write about the audacious attempt to bring about change. For if all had been as it should in Equatorial Guinea, it would have laid dormant within world attention; we would know little about those who live and suffer under its brutal regime and who try to exist in such an extreme environment. This book is not so much a sensational story of mercenary daring-do, but an overall picture of a country ruled by a corrupt dictator and whose murky history made it ripe for picking by those whose reputation was equally dubious.

That is why I have explored the past of Equatorial Guinea as well as its more contemporary and explosive events. This is a book based on facts, for all those involved – both the hunters and their prey – have conflicting stories to tell. Simon Mann and his coup team claim they were attempting to right a great wrong. Some, despite strong evidence, deny any involvement at all. But then the country's self-proclaimed president, Teodoro Obiang Nguema, says all is well under a rule which has provoked some of the greatest condemnation of human rights ever known.

This book has been compiled from factual reports of Mann's attempted coup, his arrest, trial and imprisonment, as well as documented evidence of those implicated with him. They would, of course, rather not receive mention at all – unless it was to extol their innocence.

This story is about those who dared to involve themselves in change of a country which did not want to be changed; which did not want to find itself the focus of global interest.

But far from achieving their aim, those who embarked on the coup found that their own lives would never be the same again. The penalties were high. What was to be nicknamed the 'Wonga Coup' carried a price which could never have been anticipated. Men were at the mercy of the very man whose brutal leadership they had tried to terminate. They found themselves incarcerated in a jail where many before them had been tortured and from where opposers to the regime had mysteriously disappeared. The multi-million pound reward for their endeavours evaporated leaving all feeling cheated, some betrayed and others totally alienated from the outside world. Those, like Simon Mann, the pivotal character in the plot, who finally won freedom have been wary to talk about their ordeal. It is no wonder, for self-preservation is still paramount. They will always have to look over their shoulder. And, just like all good thrillers, there remains an element of suspense.

Chapter 1

A Mann with a Mission

He was born in an ordinary barrack town but Simon Mann was destined to be anything but an ordinary serving soldier. Just over fifty years later, Mann was to win not so much a badge of honour but the mantle of notoriety in a planned mercenary coup with worldwide repercussions and which contained all the ingredients and personalities befitting a best-selling fictional thriller. His exploits are anything but fiction, however. And Mann was to suffer heavily for his ill-conceived but sensational attempt to overthrow a government in Africa's third largest oil exporter and second most corrupt country (apparently after Chad).

Simon Francis Mann was born on 26 June 1952 in the unassuming English town of Aldershot, Hampshire, just under forty miles from London and boasting a long and historical connection with the British Army. Indeed, it is a town of 'two halves' – Aldershot and Aldershot Military Town, the latter being the location for military buildings including married quarters, army playing fields and other sporting facilities mostly centred around Queen's Avenue. The Military Town also includes Aldershot Observatory, the Aldershot Military Cemetery, the Royal Garrison and other churches and barracks for the Royal Military Police. It was once the base for the Parachute Regiment following its formation in 1940 and before its move to Colchester, Essex, in 2003. The town also used to be the headquarters for the Royal Corps of Transport and the Army Catering Corps before they merged with the Royal Logistics Corps in 1993 and made their main base at the rather grim locale of nearby Deepcut (which later became infamous for several mysterious 'suicide' deaths of young soldiers).

Aldershot Military Town attracted a keen interest from Queen Victoria and Prince Albert who watched its growth as a garrison in the 1850s. The Royal couple even had a wooden boat, *Royal Pavilion*, built there in which they often stayed when attending reviews of the Army. Around 60,000 soldiers lined up for Victoria's Jubilee Review on 21 June 1887; the line-up stretching for miles and attracting Royalty and dignitaries from all over Europe and the British Empire. It was during the Crimean War that the heathland around Aldershot expanded into an army base, with the town's population increasing from just 875 in 1851 to more than 16,000 by 1861. Over half of this was made up of military personnel.

This military quarter is quite separate from the main town of Aldershot and comes under its own jurisdiction. On 22 February 1972, it suffered one of the worst mainland IRA attacks in which seven civilian support staff were killed at the 16th Parachute Brigade headquarters. The slaughter was in 'retribution' for shootings in Derry, Ireland, which were to become known as Bloody Sunday. The outrage led to the Army Town, once open-plan, being surrounded by barbed-wire fences and army patrols.

Despite the moving out of several corps and the demolition of army buildings, with such strong military foundations – Winston Churchill was based there in the nineteenth century, along with just about every famous British soldier over the years – the encampment is still justifiably known as the 'Home of the British Army'. It was also the home of Simon Mann whom it can now add to its list of notable – some may say notorious – residents.

Simon's father, George, fares much better in reputation. He was an heir to a stake in the Watney Mann brewing empire – then known as Mann, Crossman and Paulin and one of the biggest breweries in London's East End. The brewery closed in 1979 after being bought up by Grand Metropolitan (which later merged with Guinness). While not overseeing the business, George Mann was an accomplished cricketer, once described as 'one of the last gentleman cricketers', though he was once the subject of a derisory witticism from legendary commentator John Arlott. Mann was enduring something of a thrashing by his namesake, South African leg-spinner 'Tufty' Mann and Arlott commented: 'What we are watching here is a clear case of Mann's inhumanity to Mann.' Cricket certainly ran in the family blood. George's father Francis, known as Frank, also captained England, making them one of only two father and sons to achieve this (together with Colin and Chris Cowdrey). Frank led the England team in each of his seven Test matches, winning two and drawing the other five. Cricket almanac *Wisden* said of him: 'As a captain he was ideal, zealous to a degree and considerate in all things at all times.' Like his father did in 1922, George Mann captained the England cricket team on their 1948–1949 tour of South Africa. He was chairman of the Test and County Cricket Board from 1978 to 1983, most notably during the controversy over the rebel tour which Geoff Boycott and Graham Gooch led to South Africa in 1982. It is ironic that the country which hosted worthy sporting events and courted controversy for George Mann was to have an even more dramatic impact on his son some years later. Further irony is that another of Simon Mann's future newsworthy destinations was also visited many years earlier by his father. While sailing past the Gulf of Guinea, George Mann met the woman who was to be his wife – South African heiress Margaret Marshall Clarke. Simon was born as his father returned by ship to London following a South African cricket tour. George Mann had to contend with his son's dubious lifestyle and business for many years. But he did not have to bear the further angst of seeing him arrested and imprisoned. He died in 2001, three years before Simon made worldwide news, with the Royal Family sending a representative to his memorial service at the Guards Chapel at the Wellington Barracks in London.

It was not only cricket that linked the generations, but military service too. Francis Mann fought in the First World War and George served in the Scots Guards in the Second World War, winning both the Distinguished Service Order and the Military Cross and also the accolade as 'the best regimental officer in the British Army.'

It is no wonder that Simon followed the same route – that is until he sought greater excitement than the regular army could offer him.

Simon Mann enjoyed a privileged life. Following in family tradition, he was signed up to the London gentleman's club White's when he was old enough. Like most clubs of its kind, White's is steeped in tradition of gentry appeal. Founded in 1693 by Italian immigrant Francesco Bianco (AKA Francis White) this elite club was originally at 4 Chesterfield Street and sold hot chocolate – a rare and expensive treat at the time. Such places were deemed as 'hotbeds of dissent' by Charles II but many developed into respectable gentlemen-only clubs. White's later moved to 37–38 St James's and from 1783 was the unofficial headquarters of the Conservative Party. Like many haunts of the privileged, White's had its idiosyncrasies. The table in front of the club's bow window became THE place to sit; a 'throne' for the most socially influential male members, including Regency dandy Beau Brummel who was succeeded by his friend and fellow Regency buck Lord Alvanley in 1816. There is a tale that from this very chair Alvanley placed a £3,000 bet – a quite considerable amount of the time – with a friend as to which of two raindrops would first reach the bottom of a pane of glass in the bow window. White's 'betting book' also logs wagers on political affairs, especially during the tumultuous years of the French Revolution and the Napoleonic Wars. There were also social bets, such as whether a friend would marry this year, or whom. Members of White's have included Oswald Mosley, founder of the British Union of Fascists, writer Evelyn Waugh, actor David Niven and politicians Randolph Churchill and Christopher Soames. One of White's former Chairmen was Ian Cameron, father of Prime Minister David who was also a member but resigned after 15 years in 2008 saying he did not agree with the club's refusal to admit women. It is rumoured he still visits the club however. With its colourful history, White's, therefore, is highly conducive to privileged rebels like Simon Mann – whose other haunts included upper-crust nightclubs Tramps and Annabel's.

Another family tradition was maintained when Mann was sent to become one of the 1,300 pupils at Eton. But here the established Mann family futures came to a halt, leading to many arguments between Mann and his father. Although he showed early military interest by joining the cadets, Mann became a 'wet bob', preferring rowing to cricket. (Eton College owns the 2,000m lake, venue for the 2012 Olympic Rowing Regatta.) Lifelong friend Henry Bellingham who went on to become Tory MP for northwest Norfolk told *The Times*: 'He was a very charming and gregarious guy. He was very good at games and took the cadet force very seriously. He was known as "Maps" Mann because he always had maps in his hand. He was very restless, always looking for a challenge.' Bellingham claimed Mann was 'a heroic figure lacking academic ability and hankering for an active life.'

This is indeed true. For even in these early days, Simon Mann was showing some of the dangerous, daredevil thoughts which were to be his downfall in adult life. One classmate said Mann was forever planning African coups as he sat at the back of class.

When Mann left Eton it was not to go on to university but to go into the services. It seems he may not have used his time at the college to the best academic advantage. And it is doubtful he really enjoyed being amongst the sons of politicians, aristocrats and the wealthy, provoked instead, into being a rebel and fighting against the school's rules and regulations. Whatever, it is unlikely Mann would have fitted in. Former Etonian David Thomas says of the school: 'It's a name that has long carried connotations of grotesque privilege, chinless wonders and arrogant young men who deserve a good hiding ... the notion that Etonians are all idiotic twits is the first mistake the school's enemies make. In fact, Eton is a ruth-lessly efficient machine for producing tough, super-confident, often arrogant young men who are geared for success and absolutely certain that they can get it.'

On 16 December 1972 Mann won a commission into the 'family' regiment of the Scots Guards, the one in which Mann's father had so distinguished himself. It is a regiment associated with Royalty and upper-class British society. Its origins lie in the personal bodyguard of King Charles I and it can be traced back to 1642, but it was only placed on the English Establishment (becoming part of the British Army) in 1686. Bearing the nicknames 'The Kiddies' and 'Jock Guards' the regiment has as its motto *Nemo Me Impune Lacessit* – 'No one assails me with impunity'. By its own admission, the regiment is 'fiercely proud' of its 'unbroken service and loyalty to the Monarch' and its 'hard-won reputation as fighting soldiers.'

Mann gained entry to Sandhurst Academy, bastion of elite army officers. It opened in 1947 on the site of the former Royal Military College (RMC) at Sandhurst and has as its motto 'Serve to Lead'. The commissioning course lasts forty-four weeks and must be successfully completed by all British regular army officers before they receive their commission and is usually followed by a further training course specific to the regiment or corps the officer will serve in. A shorter commissioning course, run for professionally qualified officers such as doctors and chaplains, has the nickname the 'Vicars and Tarts' course. Sandhurst's stated aim is to be the 'national centre of excellence for leadership, and former officers there include Sir Winston Churchill. Two of its 'black sheep' are shamed Royal escort James Hewitt along, some agree, with Simon Mann. Nevertheless Mann excelled in the Scots Guards and by 1976 held the rank of lieutenant. But he did not find the regular Army enough of a challenge and he underwent the gruelling endurance tests required to join the SAS, the army's special-forces unit – passing first time. Rising quickly through the ranks to become a troop commander on G Squadron 22 SAS, Mann went on to serve in Cyprus, Germany, Canada, Norway, Central America and Northern Ireland.

After a standard three-year stint he returned to the regular army, completing a tour of Northern Ireland in the 1970s before postings to West Germany, Norway, Cyprus, Canada and Central America.

But in the 1980s army life began to pall. 'He had the making of a brilliant wartime general. He was very well read in military history, politics and philosophy; but peacetime soldiering was not big enough for him,' recalls Bellingham. A former colleague agrees, adding: 'I think he wanted a new challenge and after a while some people find army life a bit mundane.' Others described Mann as 'poker-faced, mysterious and secretive.' But perhaps these traits were what were needed in the life Mann had decided for himself.

Chapter 2

Secret Forces at Work

Mann left the services in 1981, aged twenty-nine. He used his SAS background to build up a business providing bodyguards to wealthy clients and also sold computer security equipment. He returned to the forces briefly in 1990 to work alongside Britain's Gulf War commander, General Peter de la Billiere.

After leaving the SAS Mann teamed up with a former insurance broker who had pioneered computer insurance and had been a manager for Control Risks, a large and reputable risk assessment consultancy that was founded by ex-SAS officers. The company described itself as an 'independent, specialist risk consultancy' providing 'advice and services that enable our clients to accelerate opportunities and manage strategic and operational risks. With 31 offices worldwide and a diverse team of consultants who are all experts in their respective fields, Control Risks offers consultancy, advice and assistance to a diverse range of corporate, governmental and non-governmental clients worldwide.'

The two men then raised finance and founded a company called Data Integrity. Mann's role was to sell new lines of computer insurance policies against accidents and hackers. The company did well, but not well enough for the venture capitalists who had funded it. It began to drift, and Mann began to lose interest. He left the directorship of Date Integrity plc and Data Integrity (Holdings) Ltd in 1989. Mann's other early business interests included being a director of the UK companies QDQ Systems Ltd and its holding company Meridian Technology Ltd until November 1986. (One address for the company was on the second floor of 22 South Audley

Street, London where Sir David Stirling, the former SAS commander and pioneer of the concept of private armies, based his private military company, KAS on the first floor.)

As Data Integrity wound down, Mann's old-boy network had put him in touch with oil entrepreneur Tony Buckingham who also had a military background and who had been a diver in the North Sea oil industry before joining a Canadian oil company. Around this time – between April 1990 and October 1993 – Mann was also a director and shareholder of a British company called Highland Software Ltd.

In 1992 Mann set up security consultancy Executive Outcomes. This was one of more than eighteen firms including international oil, gold and diamond mining ventures, a chartered accountancy office, airline, foreign security services and an offshore financial management services operation which were managed from a glass-fronted building at 535 King's Road, London, called Plaza 107. Its sister enterprise was Strategic Resources Corporation in South Africa.

Mann's other EO associate was Eeben Barlow, a former commander of 32 Battalion (also known as Buffalo Battalion) – the premier unit of the old South African Defence Force and most feared unit by its enemies in Angola and South West Africa. It was known as 'Os terriveis' – the 'Terrible Ones' – and was later used in operations contracted in Sierra Leone, Angola and other 'difficult' locations. The soldiers were described as 'experienced, reliable, trained and often very familiar with the terrain in African wars'.

Executive Outcomes was described as the 'military wing' of Branch Energy Ltd another company it owned. But following an article in *Jane's Intelligence Review* in September 1997, the company denied that Executive Outcomes or any of its related companies was a shareholder in Branch Energy and another company, Diamond-Works. It also denied claims that Branch Energy had obtained mining concessions in Sierra Leone or elsewhere. But Branch Energy was described as 'arguably the world's first corporate army ... the advance guard for major business interests engaged in a scramble for the mineral wealth of Africa. Mercenary companies are increasingly being hired to play a direct role in controlling or changing the balance of power in Africa. Corporations provide the funds for cash strapped client governments or rebel armies and in return they are rewarded with access to strategic mineral and energy resources.'

As website *GlobalSecurity.org* described Executive Outcomes, it is 'the mercenary firm based in Pretoria, South Africa, and manned mostly by former members of the South African Defence Force, has proved to be a decisive factor in the outcome of some civil wars in Africa ... Executive Outcomes reportedly has a web of influence in Uganda, Botswana, Zambia, Ethiopia, Namibia, Lesotho and South Africa ... The intermixing of paramilitary and commercial ventures makes it difficult to determine the number of mercenaries involved in various countries. Most reports indicate there were between 150 and 200 in Sierra Leone, while reports from Angola vary, indicating between 500 and 4,000 members in that country. At any rate, Executive Outcomes has proven to be a sound investment for the governments of Angola and Sierra Leone. Those successes may help to persuade other countries in the region to employ the firm's services. Increased involvement in regional security problems and an expanded portfolio of affiliated businesses suggest that Executive Outcomes will play a periodically visible role in sub-Saharan African affairs.'

And as Johann Smith, a former South African military-intelligence officer summed up: 'You had all these guys who had fought for apartheid suddenly without work when the apartheid era ended. They needed something to do. It took just four phone calls to get a battalion assembled. Still does.'

Mann was now on the edge of the dangerous life he found so enticing; the first serious steps into the rather murky world of mercenaries. For the consultancy earned a formidable reputation delivering and supplying soldiers and armed guards to businesses operating in areas of conflict. Most of EO's 1,000 or so black and white soldiers were veterans of South Africa's four elite apartheid-era counter insurgency special forces: 32 Buffalo Battalion; the Reconnaissance Commandos ('Reccies'); the Parachute Brigade ('Parabats'); and the paramilitary 'Koevoet' ('Crowbar').

It was a profitable field to be in, with Executive Outcomes earning millions from one troubled country alone. That was Angola whose government called on Mann's team of guards to protect oil installations against rebel attacks. Critics of the company were quick to point out that Buckingham was also a chief executive of a company called Heritage Oil and Gas, which had drilling interests in Angola.

Blighted with a troubled history, Angola's savage civil war had started when Angolan nationalists based in other countries and supported by the USA and Russia, declared independence and started a guerrilla campaign. The Portuguese Colonial War, which included the Angolan War of Independence, lasted until the Portuguese Colonial regime was overthrown in 1975 by a military coup in Lisbon. More than 300,000 ethnic Portuguese Angolans fled, leaving behind a country with a population mainly composed of indigenous peoples backed by three main guerrilla movements, the Popular Movement for the Liberation of Angola (MPLA), the National Union for the Total Independence of Angola (UNITA) and the National Liberation Front of Angola (FNLA). Being sympathetic to South Africa, UNITA let South African forces maintain bases in its territory for raids into Namibia or South West Africa. By the early 1980s, UNITA guerrillas had extended their control to central and southeast Angola and won the support of Great Britain, France, the United States, Saudi Arabia, and a number of African nations, while the MPLA was backed by the Soviet Union and Cuba.

In 1993, UNITA rebels seized the port of Soyo and closed its oil installations. It was this that had president Jose Eduardo dos Sontos calling on Mann for support to seize back the port. It is not surprising that throughout all this, Angola wanted to protect its oil fields. With its production potential realised in 1966, oil is the lifeblood of the government and makes up ninety per cent of the country's export revenue. After the 1975 independence national oil company the Sociedade Nacional de Combustiveis de Angola or Sonangol, was set up to manage all fuel production and distribution. The industry is still growing.

But the continual warfare disrupted Angola's economy and displaced one-sixth of its people, many of whom were forced to become refugees in Zaire, Zambia, and the Congo. In short, the conflict was one of the most notorious cold wars ever. It finally ended with a peace deal on 4 April 2002. But it was lucrative for Mann and his company. Led by Lafras Luitingh, a former 5 Recognaissance Regiment Officer, less than 100 EO fighters seized back Soyo in three months and handed it back to the Angolan government. After their successful exploits in Angola, they were offered a deal worth $80m plus diamond-mining concessions to pursue the war against UNITA and help train the national army.

In 1995, Mann and another former Scots Guard, Lieutenant-Colonel Tim Spicer, set up an offshoot company called Sandline International. Spicer is a veteran of Northern Ireland (he was awarded an OBE after his service there), The Falklands and Bosnia.

Sandline advertised its services thus:

Sandline International is a Private Military Company (PMC) which specialises in problem resolution and the provision of associated consulting services.

The business was established in the early 1990s to fill a vacuum in the post cold war era. Our purpose is to offer governments and other legitimate organisations specialist military expertise at a time when western national desire to provide active support to friendly governments, and to support them in conflict resolution, has materially decreased, as has their capability to do so.

Sandline is a privately owned and independent business. It is incorporated in the Bahamas and maintains representative offices in London, England and Washington, DC in the United States.

Mission

To provide our clients with the best possible military services in order to assist them with solving security issues quickly, efficiently and with minimum impact.

Policy

Sandline's operating principles ensure that the company only accepts projects which, in the view of its management, would improve the state of security, stability and general conditions in client countries. To this end the company will only undertake projects which are for:

- Internationally recognised governments (preferably democratically elected)
- International institutions such as the UN
- Genuine, internationally recognised and supported liberation movements – and which are – legal and moral
- Conducted to the standards of first world military forces. Where possible, broadly in accord with the policies of key western governments

13

- Undertaken exclusively within the national boundaries of the client country.

Sandline will not become involved with:

- Embargoed regimes
- Terrorist organisations
- Drug cartels and international organised crime
- Illegal arms trading
- Nuclear, biological or chemical proliferation
- Contravention of human rights
- Any activity which breaches the basic Law of Armed Conflict.

In the absence of a set of international regulations governing Private Military Companies, Sandline has adopted a self-regulatory approach to the conduct of our activities. This includes a rigid adherence to the principles outlined above. Security and confidentiality are essential and we address this in more depth below.

Management and Resources
Sandline is privately managed by a number of senior ex-military personnel from the UK and US armed forces. This management team is supported by access to a pool of consultants with extensive international commercial and legal expertise. Sandline personnel are highly professional, often former military, police and government employees, recruited from a number of countries. They are the best available, and have extensive experience of all levels of conflict, but are tuned to the nuances and political sensitivities in the world today.

All employees are thoroughly vetted by the company prior to employment and their activities are monitored closely at all times. Any breaches of discipline and confidentiality result in dismissal and may result in prosecution in the client country. Our employees operate in a hierarchical and disciplined structure, observing international laws and customs as well as those of the host country.

Operational Capability
We are able to adapt the capabilities of the company to address the legitimate requirements of our clients. The core skills of the company include:

14

Advisory
- Strategic, operational and tactical planning
- Operational research and analysis
- Independent defence reviews
- Armed forces restructuring
- Structural reviews
- Threat analysis
- Project estimates.

Training
- Basic and advanced tri-service general military training
- Special forces, Psy ops and intelligence training
- Special police unit training
- Humanitarian and disaster relief operational training
- Mine clearance training.

Operational Support
Sandline can provide specialist individuals or formed units to support a client's own armed forces on operations – typical support functions are:

- Command, control, communication and intelligence teams
- Special forces units (including counter terrorist and counter narcotic)
- Heliborne reaction forces
- Maritime special warfare units
- Pilots and engineers
- Fire support co-ordination teams
- Body guard/close protection teams
- Logistics
- Election securing/monitoring
- Integration/demilitarisation of warring factions.

Intelligence Support
- Provision of electronic, photographic and human intelligence gathering capabilities and information analysis
- Design and implementation of intelligence gathering structures and the associated training of local civilian or military personnel in intelligence operations

Humanitarian Operations
- Securing strategic assets – water, food, electricity, key installations
- Convoy escort
- Humanitarian and disaster relief command and co-ordination
- Mine clearance
- Protection of aid agency personnel
- Medical support at all levels
- Air support
- Water purification

Strategic Communications
- Public relations
- International lobbying
- Political analysis
- Psy ops
- Secure electronic communication
- Support for Law and Order

Sandline can assist in non-conflict support to law and order. Typical areas are:

- Counter-narcotics programmes
- Counter-terrorism
- Combating organised crime
- Protection of natural resources and key installations
- Anti-poaching operations
- Anti-smuggling operations
- Revenue protection
- Fisheries protection and maritime surveillance.

Project Approach
We take care to examine and analyse the issues to be addressed in considerable depth prior to any significant deployment of our personnel. This sometimes requires the completion of a consulting exercise as a preliminary exercise. A typical sequence of project management steps includes:

- Full presentation on capabilities
- Outline evaluation of the issues
- Preparation and delivery of proposal

- Contractual arrangements put in place
- Engagement of the company
- Detailed analysis of problem
- Thorough project plan worked up and agreed
- Deployment of Sandline resources
- Completion of project
- Withdrawal of project team.

Confidentiality

Sandline's projects are generally sensitive in nature and, therefore, we apply strict rules of confidentiality to our work and client relationships. These rules are reflected in our contractual obligations, corporate code and employment terms.

Our code of confidentiality is absolute. Our security procedures are rigorously enforced to ensure protection both for the client and ourselves.

Why Use Sandline?

- An independent analysis of a problem is required
- National security or stability may be threatened
- Indigenous capabilities may be insufficient
- International support is not forthcoming, but external support is essential
- Sandline supplements the local resources
- National capability is enhanced
- Appropriate actions can now be taken
- Problem expediently and cost effectively resolved.

Financial Arrangements

We offer a cost-effective solution for our clients. The financial package is self-contained and invariably determined in advance of service delivery. We anticipate all the likely operational cost sassociated with the conduct of a project and can, therefore, provide a firm figure prior to entering into a contractual arrangement. Contrary to speculation in the press, we do not seek to be rewarded in the form of mineral concessions or other indigenous assets. All Sandline contracts have addressed the issue of remuneration in an exclusively monetary form.

Summary

Sandline International is unique in its field. We have rivals but they cannot or do not wish to deploy the full range of capabilities that we offer our clients.

Our operations are completely self contained, highly disciplined and we are conscious of client confidentiality and local sensitivities. We do not always focus on the direct application of military force but are concerned with the application of a more subtle or oblique approach and, where required, the company is capable of conducting humanitarian operations.

We seek to provide training for local forces, generating a transfer of our skills which enables client governments to become self-supporting after the withdrawal of the company's personnel on the conclusion of our contract.

We are capable of very rapid deployment and operate in a cost-effective manner. We are confident that the cost to a client of deploying a Sandline project team is invariably cheaper than the cost of sourcing alternate forms of external assistance.

Sandline International operated mostly in Angola and Sierra Leone and became notorious for shipping arms to Sierra Leone in breach of a United Nations embargo. The two men claimed they were acting with the knowledge of the British Government. This was denied by the then Foreign Secretary Robin Cook. At one point Sandline became the focus of an investigation by Britain's Customs and Excise department over the arms shipment. Spicer told a press conference in London: 'If we believe our actions have the blessing of the government, as represented by officials, it's pretty galling then to be investigated as part of a criminal investigation. I did the right thing for the right guy, and with approval, but I don't have it in writing.'

According to Michael Gove of *The Times*, Mann's mercenaries helped defeat the rebels led by Forday Sankoh and laid the ground for 'democratic rule'. He argued that Mann's security businesses 'have been scrupulous about operating in concert with Western policy goals while maintaining a discreet distance.' Like most of Mann's dealings this 'logistical support' was shrouded in speculation. Mann's troops repeatedly went into action between 1983 and 1996. It was a sophisticated army available for hire by the highest bidder, though its leaders took care to choose clients favoured by western governments. But mercenaries were losing favour and Nelson Mandela's government made it illegal to offer military aid overseas.

In January 1997 EO subcontracted Sandline to provide aircraft, equipment and training to the Papua New Guinea Defence Force. EO arrived in early February and began conducting training sessions at the Urimo base near Wewak in East Sepik province.

The country's then prime minister, Sir Julius Chan's argument for hiring professionals was simple; his own military had failed over the previous eight years to put down the secessionist Bougainville Revolutionary Army. In June 1996, the Papa New Guinea government had ordered an offence, Operation High Speed 2, which was a complete failure. In September that year, eleven PNGDF troops were killed and five captured in a skirmish at Kangu beach. On 13 October, Bougainville interim government premier Theodore Miriung was assassinated. A subsequent PNG colonial inquiry implicated the PNGDF and pro-PNGDF guerrillas in his death. Defending his call on Sandline's services, Chan said: 'We have requested the Australians support us in providing the necessary specialist training and equipment. They have constantly declined and therefore I had no choice but to go to the private sector.' The fee for EO's services was set at $36m.

However, before offensive operations could commence, PNGDF Army chief Brigadier-General Jerry Singirok refused to cooperate and called for the resignation of the Prime Minister. The ensuing power struggle brought the country to the brink of civil war and did indeed culminate in the Prime Minister's resignation. Meanwhile, the EO Special Forces, temporarily detained by the defence forces they were supposed to train, slipped quietly out of the country. Sandline director Spicer was detained on guns charges to guarantee his participation in a commission of inquiry investigating the affair

On 16 April 2004, Sandline announced the closure of its operations and made a statement: 'The general lack of governmental support for Private Military Companies willing to help end armed conflicts in places like Africa, in the absence of effective international intervention, is the reason for this decision. Without such support the ability of Sandline to make a positive difference in countries where there is widespread brutality and genocidal behaviour is materially diminished.'

It seemed that by the end of 1997, Mann was ready to quit the life as mercenary overseer. Now incredibly wealthy he went into semi-retirement but the quiet life was not for him. On one occasion he sought a diversion by accompanying Buckingham on a marathon car race from China to Europe. But the two men got fed up with each other's company and went their separate ways before the race was over. A friend said of Mann's lack of racing enthusiasm: 'I've never seen anyone look so bored.' Mann no doubt got even more bored when he had to undergo surgery for a hip-replacement.

According to the Land Registry, that year he bought a manor house, 'Inchmery', a former residence of the Rothschild banking family. The eighteenth-century house in the tiny village of Exbury in Hampshire was once owned by the Mitford family and former Governor General of Australia, Lord Forster, before becoming one of the Rothschild's established homes in 1912. Lionel de Rothschild moved there with plans to create gardens in the land surrounding the house but instead purchased the neighbouring 2,000 acre Exbury Estate in 1919, which now boasts the reputation as a world-famous garden. Inchmery House itself is set in a 200 acre plot in Inchmery Lane overlooking the Solent, and was purchased by Mann in the name of Myers Developments Inc, a firm registered in the offshore Channel Islands tax haven of Guernsey. Soon after the purchase Mann advertised it with the words, 'Is this the most beautiful beach house in the country?' to secure the right tenant. He was then on the move again. Inchmery House was once valued at over £5m.

Mann's personal life had been just as demanding as his 'professional' one. He became estranged from his family when he abruptly left his first wife Jenny Barham – a member of the family who own the Hole Park estate and celebrated gardens near Tenterden in Kent – and three children. Jenny went on to marry landowner Richard Schuster. Mann then had a chance meeting in 1992 with Amanda Freedman, the tall glamorous daughter of a north London accountant Maurice and his wife Marilyn. She was the launch manager of well-known Covent Garden restaurant Christopher's and met Mann when he called in to dine there. Mann was said to be bowled over by Amanda, who later left the restaurant to become an interior designer. She said the two had fallen instantly in love and that Mann is 'an incredible romantic'. He proposed to Amanda in the Caribbean and presented her with a ring engraved with the moon and stars which he had designed himself. They married in November 1995 at Chelsea register office, not without some opposition from Amanda's family who wanted her to find a husband from a Jewish background – and certainly not a mercenary – and from Mann's who would have preferred him to find a second wife from a similar background as the first. Amanda was four months pregnant with the couple's first child Freddy. Later would come Lilly, Bess and Arthur – the latter born when Mann was in jail. Reversal of a vasectomy enabled the smitten Mann to produce these four children (it was an operation he liked to tell friends about in graphic detail).

In 1997 the Manns bought a Cape Dutch gabled house at 18 Duckitt Avenue in the exclusive Cape Town suburb of Constantia. The couple settled in quickly, spending their leisure time fishing and buying art and entertaining the many friends they had gained in their active social life. The Manns may have been happy but his family was not. Amanda would forever be considered unsuitable in their social circle (even though the Manns enjoyed Christmas dinner with neighbours Earl Spencer (Princess Diana's brother), Mark Thatcher and his ex-prime minister mother Margaret. But it was this friendship with Mark Thatcher that was to form an explosive ingredient of Mann's infamy). The family also argued about Amanda's extravagant spending – she allegedly had monthly credit card bills of £15,000 – a trait, they later said, which led to Mann's decision to embark on the infamous coup attempt in Equatorial Guinea.

But said Amanda: 'Simon never discussed his business with me. I am not a "heavy" wife. He wanted me to be at home in the traditional role of wife and mother, and I was happy to do it. He travelled a lot but he included me in his travels. He would go off to Paris and say, "I'll be there for three days, come out for one of them." He lived in Russia for three months and I went to visit him several times. It wasn't a nine-to-five job. Simon would go away a lot but when he came home he loved our family life. He would help Freddy with his times tables, and take him off fishing. He is an unbelievably fantastic father. Wherever he was on his travels, he always made it abundantly clear that me and the children are the

most important thing to him, he has always put us above everything. I feel this incredible support from him.'

Mann emerged into the limelight in 2002 to play a British officer
in Bloody Sunday, a film about Northern Ireland's 'Bloody Sunday'
killings in January 1972 when a protest march in Derry led by civil
rights activist Ivan Cooper was fired upon by British troops leaving
13 people dead and 14 wounded. The film, a documentary-style
drama, showed the events leading up to the march and starred
James Nesbitt as Cooper, Tim Piggott-Smith and James Hewitt
(best known for his liaison with Princess Diana) as Colonel Tugwell.
Mann played Colonel Derek Wilford the British commander in
charge when the killings took place and was also listed in the film
credits as a military advisor. The film's director Paul Greengrass,
described Mann as a 'humane man, but an adventurer ... very
English, a romantic, tremendously good company.' Others who
worked on the film were impressed by Mann's upper-class manners
and speech with one saying he was 'quite charming, not too
dominating.' During the filming Mann wore rimless glasses and
introduced a strong military presence on the set. One journalist
commented: 'He is straight-backed, tanned and talks like an officer.
Equivocation offends him.'

It was in the summer of 2003, that Mann met Severo Moto,
opposition leader of Equatorial Guinea, who was living in exile in
Madrid, Spain. By the end of that meeting Mann had agreed to
recruit a mercenary force to overthrow Equatorial Guinea's president
Obiang Nguema Mbasogo. It was an offer, despite its obvious
dangers – and the fact that Mann's wife was pregnant at the time –
that Mann could not refuse. The deal was a £10m fee plus a share in
future oil revenues and thirty per cent of all assets recovered from
the Obiang family. Back home in South Africa, Mann found two
friends who were willing to join him; Crause Steyl, a pilot who had
worked for him on previous operations, and Nick du Toit, a former
officer in the South African Special Forces. Steyl was delegated to
organise all the air transport and du Toit to help with recruiting and
setting up 'logistical support' in Equatorial Guinea. Another recruit
was a businessman later said to be the leading financial backer of the
coup. Denying his involvement, the man cannot be named in any
connection to Simon Mann or the attempted coup. There was a
fourth 'main man' – Mark Thatcher (son of former British Prime

22

Minister Margaret Thatcher), later alleged to have paid for the purchase of a plane and whose subsequent arrest was to make news worldwide. Mann said that he had held several meetings about the coup with du Toit, and that in November 2003, made the phone calls to recruit former Executive Outcomes soldiers. Recruitment meetings took place at a hotel in Pretoria, known as the '224' because of the number of rooms it has.

But to the outside world and even to his friends, it seemed Mann had apparently finally settled down and withdrawn from his dangerous and dubious profession ... until the shock news reached his friends that he had been arrested at Zimbabwe's Harare airport on 7 March 2004.

Chapter 3

A Coup de Farce

Mann had gone to meet sixty-six South African soldiers and three crew who had flown in from America in a Boeing 727 owned by another of Mann's companies, Logo Logistics. They carried bolt-cutters, pepper spray and sledgehammers on board and their mission was to later take on £100,000 worth of ammunition. Severo Moto was already on his way to the African desert, flying in under the radar. The plan was for him to be installed in Equatorial Guinea the next day.

All seemed to be going well with Customs officers copying the men's passports and asking no difficult questions about their reasons for being in the country. It was, however, a carefully-worked out plan to ensure all the men involved could be easily rounded-up.

And Mann was not on his own as he waited on the tarmac for the 727 to land. Waiting too, was a troop of Zimbabwean soldiers armed with twenty light machine guns, sixty assault rifles, fifty heavy machine guns, 100 grenade launchers and more than 100,000 rounds of ammunition. Police swarmed on to the plane and in what must have seemed like moments for Mann and his team, the planned coup had suffered a coupe de grâce – but one which would prove to be anything but merciful.

They had fallen into a trap. They had also fallen into the hands of soldiers and police officers who had no qualms about serving out a beating. More beatings would follow at the police station. Said Mann: 'We were roughed up and then roughed up some more. Then we were thrown into a real shit of a holding cell.' In short, Mann and his men were under the jurisdiction of President Robert Mugabe's security force.

The news of his arrest reached his distraught wife back home. She described it all to Natalie Clarke of the *Daily Mail*: 'I had kissed him goodbye and said: "Be home, be safe." We spoke by phone after he left and I think the last time I spoke to him was one day in early March. A few days later, I got the call at 7am from one of Simon's contacts. He said that Simon's plane was in Zimbabwe but there was no sign of Simon, they couldn't find him. I remember my blood turning cold and I said, "Has there been an accident?" My first thought was that the plane had crashed. Everything happened in slow motion that morning. I took the children to school as usual and tried to deal with the job in hand, but my heart was racing. Over the next twenty-four hours I continually phoned his mobile but it just rang out.

'The next day, I phoned one of Simon's special friends, one of his contacts in the security business, and said Simon was missing and he said he would look out for him. Two days after that, he called back to say that Simon was in a Zimbabwean prison. It was such a relief to learn he was alive, and although it was a shock to hear he was in prison, I thought, well, it will be sorted out, he will be released at some point.'

In all, seventy men were arrested including Nick du Toit and seven others who were waiting in the Equatorial Guinea city of Malabo. They were all charged with violating the country's immigration, fire-arms and security laws. They were later to be accused of involve-ment in an attempted coup in Equatorial Guinea. One was later to die in prison. Crause Steyl, waiting in Mali for word that the coup was a success before flying into Equatorial Guinea with Severo Moto, escaped arrest. He later said he felt he had been shadowed on the day of the coup attempt and was then told he should 'just disappear.' Severo Moto was immediately flown back to Spain.

Also arrested were Hermanus Carlse and Lourens Horn, two owners of the company Meteoric Tactical Solutions (MTS), who had arrived the day before as an 'advance party' tasked with collecting the weapons. MTS was a South African private military company with a $492,764 contract with the British Department for International Development to provide bodyguards and drivers for the most senior officials in Iraq in the summer of 2003. The company also had a contract with the Pentagon to train the new Iraqi police force as well as a $1.3m contract from the Swiss government to protect their missions in Iraq in early summer 2004. At that time, the DFID was criticised by members of the House of Commons for not vetting MTS thoroughly enough. Carlse and Horn were acquitted that August of the charges linking them to the coup but when they arrived home in South Africa, they pleaded guilty to violating the Foreign Military Assistance Act and received reduced sentences for agreeing to testify at Thatcher's trial into his part in the coup. The unwanted attention on MTS resulted in the loss of many contracts set up in Iraq by the company's third owner, Festus van Rooyen, and was forced to close down. Van Rooyen said he had had nothing to do with the Equatorial Guinea attempted coup but commented: 'Ironically, those of us who are trying to do things legally are getting the most flack from the government. The guys working under the table have no problems.'

On 25 March 2004, it was claimed in the South Africa press that Mann had not been planning a coup, but had in fact, been a bounty hunter, out to get disgraced Liberian dictator Charles Taylor who had a £1.1m price on his head put up by the US Congress after he was ousted out of office in August 2003. The mercenary group had been bound for Calabar, a port in south-east Nigeria to snatch Taylor, hand him over to the war crimes authorities and split the money.

On 11 May a group of around 150 black and white protestors and including women and children, gathered on the lawns of Pretoria's Union Buildings, the seat of the South African Government. The group were relatives and friends of the arrested mercenaries and after two long months, they now wanted South Africa to intervene in the mens' plight. They sang the national anthem and carried placards that read 'Bring Them Back!' and 'What about human rights?' in reference to the fifteen men behind bars in Equatorial Guinea and the others in prison in Zimbabwe.

One of the protestors was Nick du Toit's wife Belinda who wept as she handed over a petition to a junior South African government official. She told the BBC: 'I hope someone in the South African government will listen to our pleas. If our men must be tried let it happen here where there is a fair, legal system. If they stay where they are now, I'm sure they won't get a fair trial.'

Soon after Mann was arrested, British MPs started to ask questions in the House of Commons about his welfare – and involvement in the attempted coup. On 20 May, 2004, Conservative MP for Worthing

West, Peter Bottomley, was one of those who raised the issue to Jack Straw, the Secretary of State for Foreign and Commonweath Affairs as reported in Commons' record Hansard:

(1) what information he has assessed on the treatment of Mr Simon Mann in Zimbabwe;
(2) whether the authorities in Zimbabwe have indicated that they consider Mr Simon Mann to be British;
(3) what representations he has made about the treatment of Mr Simon Mann and his condition.

He was answered by Labour MP for Harlow, Bill Rammell, Parliamentary Under-Secretary, Foreign and Commonwealth Office: 'Mr Simon Mann is a dual British/South African national who requested our consular assistance on 23 April. Our rules on consular confidentiality mean that we cannot discuss the specific details of his case. However, the Zimbabwean authorities recognised his nationality status by allowing our Consul to visit him on 7 May, where we were able to discuss his welfare and treatment. We welcomed the Zimbabwean court's decision on 7 May to remove handcuffs and manacles from all of the accused while they are detained in Chikurubi Prison, Harare. We will continue to be guided by Mr Mann about his treatment and are in regular contact with his lawyers and family.'

Initially, after Mann's arrest, he and Amanda wrote to each other every week. But it was a heartbreaking time for them both, and Amanda knew she had to keep strong. 'He used to write me love letters from his prison cell. People asked me how I coped and it was because he has always put me first. I didn't ask him about the conditions in jail, I couldn't because I needed to preserve some space in my heart to exist. One piece of advice I had from a dear friend of Simon's was that in order to keep Simon well, I mustn't come over too emotional. So I kept my letters relatively upbeat, talking about what the children were up to. We have a secret language, so I would put in a few lines so he would know it was me. He used to write that he was so looking forward to reading the words, "Welcome to Heathrow."'

Amanda said that in a way her being pregnant actually helped because it made her feel closer to Simon. She eventually gave birth at home because she felt there would be too much emotional stress

27

in hospital. 'One of the most painful things I have ever done in my life was phoning up Simon's lawyer in Zimbabwe the next day and saying to him, "Last night I had a baby boy, we are all fine and Simon must name our child." He'd named our other children and this was to be no different. The message came back "Arthur". It was so unbelievably emotional. I did not go to Zimbabwe because Simon did not want me to. He didn't want our love to be shattered by the emotional pain we would both suffer if I saw him in jail. And what if something happened to me in this unlawful country? I have four children who need their mother.'

Amanda said that 'everyone loved' her 'true gentleman' husband in jail and that he taught English to the guards and fellow inmates 'to help improve their lives when they were released. Everyone who meets Simon speaks highly of his human skills, the way he can connect with people of any background.'

It seems the whole coup operation was doomed from the start. (The first attempt failed when an AM-12 plane broke down and the coup was re-scheduled for 7 March 2004.) With just over two days' notice, two warships from Spain set sail towards the Gulf of Equatorial Guinea with 500 men on board. There would be speculation as to what part this was to play, but such a high-profile, coincidental presence could not help but arouse suspicions. And just like every other aspect of the disastrous plan, it provoked accusations, denials and confusion. Obiang accused the Spanish government of supporting the coup plot, saying it was funding opposition groups in exile and supporting the coup directly. He said: 'Our intelligence sources say that the warship was going to arrive on the same date that the coup attempt was going to take place – 8 March ... It [the war ships] was already in our territorial waters with 500 soldiers aboard. Meanwhile there was a team of foreign mercenaries already in Equatorial Guinea who knew where we lived. They had plans to kill fifty people and to arrest others.' The Spanish foreign ministry spokeswoman denied the allegations: 'There was no ship there; we deny any kind of implication in any attempted coup.' However the Spanish foreign minister, Ana Palacio seemed to contradict the spokeswoman's statement; saying, 'They weren't on a mission of war, but one of cooperation'.

And in regard to the landing of a plane at Zimbabwe, Mann's former business partner Greg Wales was to comment: 'Whatever

Simon was doing, he was incredibly stupid to be flying a bunch of people to Zim and picking up weapons at the same time. If you think you can do that without a problem, you are a bit naive.'

The magazine *Vanity Fair* was later to report that a London financier had told them how a 'certain oil businessman' invited him to his house in August 2003 and requested that he ask a client to invest in the coup, which he said would make them very rich because Moto had promised the backers oil concessions. According to the financier, the businessman explained that he couldn't fund the operation entirely himself, because his assets were frozen as a result of his being accused of taking kickbacks in securing oil licenses elsewhere. The businessmen said the plan was to go into Equatorial Guinea while Obiang was out of the country being treated for cancer. 'We have a mole in the hospital,' the financier was told. The businessman also allegedly stated that he had successfully done 'this sort of thing before'. The financer said he was appalled and advised his client to have nothing to do with the plan.

But how were the co-conspirators found out? It appears that their conversations were often conducted in public – sometimes as they lazed around a swimming pool – and that they could not refrain from bragging about their intentions. One meeting allegedly took place in a restaurant 'with thirty-five drunken Afrikaners roaring away to anyone who cared to listen.' Mann assumed that almost everyone would be pleased to see the back of Obiang, and that by voicing his plans abroad he was allowing Britain, the US, Spain and South Africa to know what was happening; if they didn't react he would take it that he had their tacit consent. The plotters actually told Bulelani Ngcuka, the head of South Africa's prosecution authority and a Mbeki intimate, what they were planning and again assumed that the lack of official response meant they had Mbeki's implicit permission to go ahead.

It was said that Nick du Toit's recruiting activities inevitably attracted the attention of the South African intelligence service, which alerted the governments of Britain, Spain and the US.

Some expressed incredulity at the whole scheme – and its instigation. Said one SAS source: 'It is inconceivable that an ex-SAS officer like Simon Mann would be waiting at a heavily-guarded airport to greet a bunch of unarmed mercenaries from a plane. If he was planning a destabilising operation in the country, he would

29

insert his team in one of several far more secret and effective ways and they would be armed to the teeth. These flights carrying guys destined to do security work in diamond facilities have been going on for several years.'

In December 2003 and January 2004, a former South African special forces commander (and occasional adviser to Obiang) Johann Smith, heard rumours of the planned coup and sent two highly-detailed reports about it to two senior officers in British intelligence, to Michael Westphal, a senior colleague of Donald Rumsfeld, America's Secretary of Defence, and to South African Intelligence. The documents were marked 'strictly confidential'. On the front page was a map of Equatorial Guinea, with its name and its capital Malabo written in large letters.

As author Adam Roberts said: 'A regime like Obiang's depends heavily on mercenary bodyguards, even for intelligence; and Obiang was very dependent on one Johann Smith, a South African special forces veteran, who repeatedly warned him of possible plots to impose Moto.'

Smith had teamed up with a man called Nigel Morgan – nick-named 'Nosher' and 'Captain Pig' – who had worked in a Thatcher think tank, served in the Irish Guards and then got into the private security business in the Congo, where he recruited Victor Dracula, an Angolan who had served with SA special forces and James Kershaw, a radio and computer expert. Morgan also came across Nick du Toit. 'As luck would have it, he ultimately threw his lot in with Mann, not Smith.' (But it was said that Morgan was the one who blew the whistle on the coup. He later declared to a reporter: 'My dear fellow, intelligence is what greases the wheels of this world, and that means deceit and betrayal. That's what Simon Mann was doing – deceiving the world about his intentions. It's not illegal to plan a coup or talk about it with your chums in Annabel's or White's club. But it is in South Africa. He broke his word to people I knew, my friends, that he wouldn't get involved in any of this. I was cornered. I had an obligation to tell what I knew'.)

Dracula was to spend fourteen months in Chikurubi jail after he said he was 'tricked' into joining Mann's plot. Dracula later said: 'We were told we were going to the Congo to work on security at a new mine. We were shocked when we got arrested in Harare. I was supposed to earn £2,000-a-month with bonuses. After what he put us through he has a moral duty to pay what he owes.' Dracula, like others, also balked at the treatment Mann received in jail, saying: 'He is definitely someone who gets what they want. Wardens treated him with more respect, as if he was a better class of criminal.'

Said Roberts: 'All this was to have fateful consequences. South Africa's National Intelligence Agency is stuffed full of agents who learned their craft as operatives for the ANC's armed wing, Umkhonto we Sizwe (MK), once one of the world's least-effective guerrilla forces. As a result President Mbeki still relies for anything really serious on white Afrikaners from the ancient regime, several of whom have set up private security companies with ties to mercenary and special forces circles. "Nosher" Morgan moved in these circles and supplied intelligence to Mbeki's network. A friend of both Thatcher and Mann, he realised early on what was up and inserted Kershaw as Mann's special assistant. With Kershaw reporting back to Morgan and Morgan in turn reporting to South African intelligence, the plot was no secret in Pretoria. Interestingly, Obiang and Mbeki were both to fulminate against the phenomenon of white mercenaries, but both depended on them to foil Mann's plot.'

In a statement to lawyers representing the government of Equatorial Guinea, Smith later said he began hearing rumours of a coup in both Equatorial Guinea and Sao Tomé in November 2003 from two ex-soldiers of the 32 Buffalo Battalion who told him they had been recruited for a coup by Nick du Toit.

Smith said: 'Because I was continuing to work in Equatorial Guinea with government, it was not in my interest that there be a coup d'état ... I therefore wanted to warn the Equatorial Guinea authorities. I also considered it my duty to warn the authorities in US and England because some of their nationals might be killed. I submitted a report in December 2003 of what I had discovered to Michael Westphal of the Pentagon (in Donald Rumsfeld's department). I expected the US government to take steps to warn Equatorial Guinea or to stop the coup. This was also my expectation as regard the British government, which I warned through two Special Intelligence Service (SIS) people I knew, and to whom I sent the report by email, also in December 2003, to their personal email addresses.'

One eleven-page report named several of the major players who had been arrested that March. Smith said the group had hired two fishing trawlers to operate off the West African coast, despite the fact that all but one member of the group had no seagoing or fishing experience. The report concluded that the commercial fishing operation was a front for the movement of men and arms for a coup. The report also mentioned the group's connections with the Equatorial Guinea opposition leader Severo Moto and warned that any operation would pose a threat to stability in the region. When Smith began to get more intelligence of the plot in January from his former military colleagues who were working for Nick du Toit's South African firm, he sent another report to the Pentagon and SIS marked 'strictly confidential'. He said: 'After preparing and sending my December report I received further information ... I put this in a second report, which I sent by email to the same people as the first one: Michael Westphal of the US and to British SIS contacts.'

Documents seen by the *Observer* newspaper revealed that by the end of January, the Foreign Office was being told: 'According to the latest planning, Carlos Cardoso (ex-South African special forces soldier) would, on his return, recruit a total of seventy-five ex-SADF [South African Defence Force] members, mainly from within the former 32 Buffalo's (battalions) and Special Forces ranks to launch simultaneous actions in STP and EG. These actions are planned to take place in mid-March 2004 ... Knowing the individuals as well as I do, this timeline is very realistic and will provide for ample time to plan, mobile, equip and deploy the force.'

Smith said there was no response from British or American authorities to his warnings. It was reported that the only reaction from America was to freeze the Equatorial Guinea money lodged with the US Riggs Bank. By this time, the group of mercenaries had checked into a hotel in February 2004 to await further instructions. (Smith later claimed he received death threats after the plot was thwarted, had been ambushed three times – but that 'I am still here.')

That same month, at a meeting at Chatham House (a non-profit, non-government organisation whose mission is to analyse and promote the understanding of major international issues and current affairs) attended, according to a witness, by an official from the US State Department and a diplomat from the British Foreign Office, an oil executive stood up and said: 'Everyone knows there's going to be a coup in EG led by South African mercenaries.'

The planned coup became the talk of the backstreet bar haunts of soldiers for hire. It was not long before the South African government was receiving regular updates on the proposed coup. This was all passed on to the relevant parties. Mann was later to confess he had let his team down saying: 'I carry the can for that. I was bloody stupid. *Mea culpa'* (my mistake).

It was claimed that the attempted coup coincided with – and may have contributed to – a purge of foreigners in Equatorial Guinea. Two weeks preceding it, and for weeks afterwards, up to 1,000 African nationals (mainly Cameroonians) were deported. Cameroon withdrew its ambassador in protest. Human Rights Watch interviewed a number of Ghanaians and Nigerians who had been deported from Equatorial Guinea during this purge. Several women claimed they were raped and that local Equatorial Guineans who were not police officers were allowed to arrest people suspected of being illegal residents. Many were forcibly deported without due process or being allowed to exercise their right to appeal. A small number of oil workers were also arbitrarily detained and assaulted, such as the representative of the Angolan state oil company Sonangol.

Equatorial Guinea's attorney general also issued a warning that the coup plotters 'are commandos, they are more highly trained than an ordinary military officer ... they were going to come to Equatorial Guinea under the effects of drugs, and so they were not going to have pity on anyone. Therefore, as attorney general, I call on the population to be vigilant with foreigners, regardless of colour, because the target is the wealth of Equatorial Guinea, the oil.'

Award-winning British film-maker James Brabazon later admitted he had been invited by du Toit to actually film the attack on Obiang's regime as it happened. He told the *Observer*: 'I said but this is like the plot of a book surely, and Nick leaned forward and said quite seriously "It's not like the plot of a book, it is one, Frederick Forsyth's *Dogs of War*. You should read it."'

Brabazon was later to have a good insight into exactly what had gone wrong with the attempted coup: 'Unknown to me, the apparently watertight plans for the operation had dissolved into farce of epic proportions. I learnt later that at exactly the time I'd called, Phase One of the operation had been launched – and then abandoned in what could only be described as an undignified shambles.

'Sixty-seven of Africa's most well-known mercenaries had embarked on two Dakotas at a civilian airfield in South Africa in broad daylight, while plane spotters had taken pictures of them and written down the aircraft's ID numbers. They flew to an airstrip in the Congo – which was supposed to have been secured by a local rebel group – to cross-load the weapons and ammo being brought up from Zimbabwe. Except, of course, that in time-honoured African tradition the rebels failed to show up. The mercenaries hot-footed it to neighbouring, law-abiding Zambia before the Congolese army could turn up in force. Here, they waited for seven hours at a commercial airport before flying back home again, where all sixty-seven of them were promptly installed in a cheap hotel – next door to the headquarters of the South African National Intelligence Agency. In a separate example of extraordinary timing, the aircraft that was plying the weapons run from Equatorial Guinea to Zimbabwe and then Congo was crippled shortly after take-off – and forced to make an emergency landing after its nosecone was struck by a goose ... A jet airliner would be brought in from the USA by an ex-CIA pilot, collecting the mercenaries and weapons in one flight. The President of Equatorial Guinea would be taken out in a small operation. Crucially, Nick had failed to realise that the President had given orders to liquidate local army commanders likely to be sympathetic to the coup. Our movements were scrutinised.'

According to Mann later, it was du Toit who had pushed to use Zimbabwe as the place to buy arms – the part of the plan that backfired so badly. An insider said that by early 2004, Mann was reportedly coming under pressure from his businessman backer, not least because they had already spent more than $2m of the operation's funds. According to one source, Mann did not tell some of his backers that he was picking up arms in Zimbabwe rather than in the Democratic Republic of Congo, as was the original plan. (It was said that when Mann had initially gone to the Congo in February, he had found no weapons at the allotted rendezvous.) When Severo Moto's group heard Mann had been arrested in Harare, they were stunned, with one asking: 'What the fuck is Simon doing in Zimbabwe?'

There was proving to be little honour among this gang of thieves; at least one of the architects of the coup was working as a double agent for the Equatorial Guinean government.

34

The initial claim by Mann and his co-accused was that they had no plans involving Equatorial Guinea but were on their way to the Democratic Republic of Congo to provide security for diamond mines owned by the JFPI Corporation – Africa's largest private holding company and closed-end investment (a collective investment scheme with a limited number of shares) company with global links. But after months of secretly collecting information, South African intelligence sources had their own ideas; that there were plans to seize control of Equatorial Guinea and run it as a private fiefdom modelled on the British East India Company after installing exiled opposition leader Severo Moto, and that the background businessman funded the proposed coup in exchange for offshore oil rights.

Mann was later to admit that money and business reasons were a motivation, but the primary motivation was to help the people of Equatorial Guinea who were in a lot of trouble.

Mann was taken into solitary confinement in Zimbabwe's hellhole of Chikurubi maximum-security prison. From there he wrote desperate letters to his wife, lawyer and friends asking them to contact the 'investors' in the coup mission to raise more money (knowing that in such circumstances money speaks louder than words) in a bid secure his freedom. In one he said: 'What we need is maximum effort – whatever it takes now ... It may be that getting us out comes down to a large splodge of wonga.' One of those Mann suggested approaching for help was Mark Thatcher (who Mann nicknamed 'Scratcher', apparently a reference to Thatcher's boyhood affliction of eczema), whose response was succinct when telephoned by Dries Coetzee, a private detective hired by Mann's lawyer. Thatcher said: 'Look, Mr Coetzee, I tend not to give money to people I've never met, so why don't you just fuck off.' Thatcher then reportedly went back to watching the Grand Prix race on television. Another person Mann wrote to for help was David Hart, the millionaire old Etonian who was Margaret Thatcher's chief enforcer during the 1984 strikes and who sometimes acted as a go-between in negotiations between governments and defence contractors. (Obiang was later to claim he had evidence that Hart helped finance the coup.) Mayfair property dealer Gary Hersham and South African-based Briton David Tremain were also alleged to have raised £270,000, an accusation they denied.

All these names were allegedly on a so-called 'Wonga List' handed over to South African police by James Kershaw who was believed to have acted as Mann's accountant. Kershaw entered a witness protection scheme after voluntarily surrendering to police on advice of his lawyers. He was given 24-hour police protection because of fears of assassination. In a note sent to his legal team from prison, Mann expressed disappointment at receiving no help from his 'friends'. He wrote: 'Our situation is not good and it is very URGENT. They [the lawyers] get no reply from the businessman and Scratcher asked them to ring back after the Grand Prix race was over ... we need heavy influence of that sort ... the businessman, Scratcher ... David Hart. And it needs to be used heavily and now. Once we get into a real trial scenario we are fucked.' At the end of one of the notes, Mann added: 'Anyway, (another contract) was expecting funds inwards to Logo (Mann's firm) from Scratcher (200) ... if there is not enough, then present investors must come up with more.' (The notes were obviously vetted by the South African authorities and eventually they knew just who else was implicated in the attempted coup. On 25 August, Thatcher was awoken at 3am and arrested on charges that he helped fund the plot.)

Yet another man, Mann's former business partner and London-based property dealer Greg Wales was also implicated and was said to have raised $500,000. He was later accused in the South African court of helping to plan the coup and of approaching the Pentagon for support. Wales denied it. Theresa Whelan, a member of President Bush's administration in charge of African affairs at the Pentagon said she had met Wales twice in Washington before the coup attempt. A US defence official told *Newsweek* magazine: 'Mr Wales mentioned in passing ... there might be some trouble brewing in Equatorial Guinea. Specifically, he had heard from some business associates of his that wealthy citizens of the country were planning to flee in case of a crisis.'

Others named in connection with the plot issued their own statements. Mark Thatcher, said to have funded the purchase of a plane for the coup, made the very non-committal comment: 'Simon Mann is an old friend of mine for whom I have the utmost sympathy throughout this whole ghastly process.' The business man's statement was one of denial and read: 'I confirm that I had no involvement in, or responsibility for, the alleged coup.' He had been mentioned in a signed statement by Mann after his arrest. Mann said: 'X asked me if I would like to meet Severo Moto ... I met Severo Moto in Madrid ... at this stage they asked me if I could help escort Severo Moto home at a given moment while simultaneously there would be an uprising of both military and civilians against [President Teordoro Obiang Nguema Mbasogo] ... I agreed to try and help the cause.'

In the spring of 2004, shortly after the plot was uncovered, Scotland Yard launched Operation Antara following a formal request from Equatorial Guinea that it should investigate 'the involvement of British citizens'. The claim that it was largely planned and financed from Britain was passed to Scotland Yard via the Foreign Office and Home Office.

During the court hearing, Hope Mutize, marketing manager of state owned Zimbabwe Defence Industries (ZDI) said that Mann had paid him a deposit on weapons worth $180,000 – around £100,000 – in February 2004. Mutize said Mann had been accompanied by Nick du Toit and that 'they insisted they did not want any paperwork.' Legal sources said Mann had cleared the deal with ZDI's managing director Colonel Tshinga Dube. Things got even murkier, when the *Zimbabwe Independent* reported that the sale of weapons to the coup members by ZDI was facilitated by a local businessman, Martin Bird, who allegedly introduced Mann and his team to Dube. The report said that it was understood Bird 'connected Mann and his associates to Dube for negotiations about the arms deal.' Bird and Dube were said to be long-standing business associates. Sources said that after Bird introduced Mann to Dube and other ZDI officials the deal was struck. It was claimed in court that Mutize's involvement was part of a well-orchestrated sting operation against the mercenaries and that ZDI, which supplies army uniforms, field equipment and ammunition, sold arms to the suspects without an end-user certificate. The arms included sixty-one AK-47 assault rifles and 45,000 rounds of ammunition, 300 offensive hand grenades, twenty PKM light machines guns and 30,000 rounds of ammunition, fifty PRM machine guns, and 100 RPG 7 anti-tank launchers and 1,000 rounds of ammunition.

In August 2004, Jack Straw issued a strong denial that Britain had known anything about a planned coup.

As one observer noted: 'Imprudent as the plot may have been, it has developed into a conspiracy theorist's dream, with tantalizing tentacles reaching to the upper echelons of British and American commerce and politics.'

And another source told journalists Raymond Whitaker and Paul Lashmar how the days had gone when mercenaries could walk into small African countries and take them over, saying: 'Things have changed in Africa over the past few years. The days are gone when you could recruit a bunch of moustaches, load up some ammunition and take over a country – especially if you are a white man.'

It was revealed in August too, that before his arrest, Mann had approached Gianfranco Cicogna, a South African-based telecoms tycoon and that the two men had discussed investing $200,000 in a 'project' in Equatorial Guinea. No money was handed over and Cicogna said: 'What return that would have brought, I have no idea. We were going to meet again. Nothing of this was finalised.' He added that the idea of a coup attempt had not 'crossed my mind' and that although he had seen Mann a week before he was arrested in Zimbabwe, news reports were the first he had heard about the plot.

Chapter 4

A Leading Player

South African arms dealer and former army officer Nick du Toit is the man said to have been enlisted by Simon Mann to recruit participants in the attempted coup, to supply the mercenaries with arms including AK47s, RPGs, PK machine guns and mortars, to secure the control tower at Malabo airport and change the frequency to establish communication with the incoming plane from Zimbabwe carrying more mercenaries. Du Toit was described as 'one of the leading players' but was later to say that he got involved only because he believed the British and South African governments had backed it. He served five years and eight months of his 34-year sentence in a 5ft by 7ft (150cm by 210cm) cell at the notorious Black Beach prison in Malabo.

A long-standing soldier – he was a colonel in the Reconnaissance Commando unit of apartheid South Africa's Special Forces – du Toit, like many Afrikaners who had fought on the 'wrong side' found it hard to find a place in the post-apartheid state – or indeed do anything else in life. He said: 'I have been in the military for almost twenty years, a true and proper career. Afterwards I tried to settle down and start in a business, but most of them didn't work.'

Du Toit admitted that the coup attempt appealed to him, saying: 'We liked the idea of Russian Mi-8s and Mi-17s. I had access to some being sold off by the Zambian government.'

He also talked of a meeting between him and Mark Thatcher at the Airport Sun Hotel near Johannesburg airport. 'I found him in the lounge. I had brought along a quote. We talked for a couple of hours. Simon had said it was best not to mention Equatorial Guinea.'

Within weeks, Thatcher was funding an Alouette helicopter purchased through Crause Steyl, a former military pilot who ran an air ambulance service. Thatcher's defence to charges that he breached South Africa's anti-mercenary laws by providing funds for the helicopter was that he thought he was contributing to an air ambulance. Du Toit later claimed: 'There is no doubt in my mind that Thatcher was involved with the coup plot. The guy negotiated a plea-bargain with a fine and suspended sentence and effectively got off scot-free.'

While in Black Beach jail awaiting trial, du Toit was allowed to talk to a journalist from the *London Evening Standard* newspaper. He was described in the report, published on 12 October 2004, as 'shackled and manacled, bearded and bedraggled' after seven months in the prison. Du Toit told the newspaper that he had met Thatcher through Mann. As reporter and prisoner talked, an official from Equatorial Guinea's Ministry for Security burst into the room with a laptop belonging to du Toit and demanded that he open three programmes which had been locked by a secret code. When the programmes were opened there was a list of names, headed by Simon Mann, including others connected to the attempted coup – and Thatcher's name quite high up on the list accompanied by his closely-guarded personal telephone number. But there was nothing to link Thatcher directly to the plot.

Du Toit's trial started on 16 November 2004. On 26 November he was found guilty of terrorism, crimes against the head of government and the illegal possession of arms and explosives and sentenced to thirty-four years in prison. He was also fined around 12m rand. After the trial, du Toit and the others were 'bundled into a truck like animals without even understanding what sentences they received. There was not even a translator in court when the judge gave his ruling. South African consular officials had to tell us what was going on and what the sentences were,' said du Toit's distraught wife Belinda. 'The soldiers refused to allow them to even look in our direction.'

Before the sentencing, South Africa had said it would intervene should the death penalty be meted out to du Toit. The death penalty is banned in South Africa.

Belinda and Georgia Boonzaaier, wife of fellow conspirator Bones Boonzaaier, joined forces to organise an appeal against their husbands' convictions. Said Belinda at the time: 'We have five days to decide whether we want to appeal. We have been told that if the appeal is dismissed the men might face even harsher sentences. I don't know whether to return home or not. I simply have to try and see Nick to give him food and medicine. He has flu and gets malaria every three weeks. He gets no medication. And, I want to visit him for the last time.'

One expert observer of the trial, Professor André Thomashausen of Unisa's Centre for International Law, said the men's sentences were much harsher than the international norm of a maximum of twenty-five years, and added: 'This period is based on the fact that no person can survive longer in prison. One must accept that judicial officials in Equatorial Guinea probably are not even aware of this norm.'

Lawyer Fabian Nsue Nguema said they would appeal adding: 'We want to bring to light for the whole world to see all the irregularities that have marked this trial ... the fact that the prisoners did not have free access to their lawyers and the torture that they endured in jail.'

The sham of a trial was focussed on by Amnesty International who produced a report:

Here are some of Amnesty International's observations from 26 November 2004.

EQUATORIAL GUINEA: TRIAL OF ALLEGED COUP PLOTTERS FLAWED

Eleven foreign nationals and nine Equatorial Guineans were sentenced to lengthy prison terms and hefty fines in Equatorial Guinea after a grossly unfair trial ending on 26 November 2004. They were convicted of (an attempt to commit) crimes against the Head of the State and against the government.

The Equatorial Guineans were tried in absentia. The lawyers of the foreign defendants have lodged an appeal to the Supreme Court against the convictions.

Neither the verdict nor the sentences were translated, and the defendants left court with no knowledge of their fate.

An Amnesty International delegation observed the trial from its commencement on 23 August 2004, and, in view of serious procedural flaws and the admission of confessions allegedly extracted under torture, deemed it to be unfair.

Nineteen people, including five Equatorial Guineans, six Armenians and eight South Africans, were charged with crimes against the Head of State; crimes against the government; crimes against the peace and independence of Equatorial Guinea; possession and storage of arms and ammunition; treason; possession of explosives; and terrorism, for which the prosecution had demanded the death penalty for South African Nick du Toit and prison sentences ranging from twenty-six to eighty-six years for his co-defendants.

No evidence was presented in court to sustain the charges against the accused, other than their statements, which the defendants said had been extracted under torture. However, defendants' protestations to this effect were ignored by the bench. No court can ignore allegations as serious as these. They are sufficient grounds for a trial to be suspended and an investigation to be instituted.

At the request of the prosecution, the trial was adjourned indefinitely at the end of August, ostensibly in the light of emerging evidence deemed vital to the case. However, when the trial resumed in November, no new evidence was presented in court. Instead, new names were added to the list of accused, including that of Severo Moto, a political opponent exiled in Madrid, eight members of his 'government in exile' who were tried in absentia, and several British and South African businessmen.

It is these businessmen who face proceedings in the English High Court brought by Equatorial Guinea and its UK legal adviser, Penningtons.

The last line of these observations is intriguing – and brings yet another controversial aspect to the 2004 attempted coup on Equatorial Guinea. For the country was indeed being represented by a British legal firm. Henry Page was the partner of City law firm Penningtons and was acting as an adviser to Obiang. The connection was investigated in February 2005 by the publication *Legal Business* whose reporter Anthony Notaras commented: 'The plot that surrounds the attempted African coup d'état has all the makings of a grisly, hugely unpleasant spectacle. Torture is being alleged. People are suffering. By any standards, it's an almighty mess. A 52-year-old partner from Penningtons, a respected City-based English law firm, is in the eye of the storm.' The report went on to note: 'The legal fall-out from the attempt to overthrow the president of Equatorial Guinea has turned into a bitter affair. It raises issues as to how UK lawyers should deal with instructions when faced with such complex clients and allegations, and how much weight can be attached in the English courts to evidence gathered in circumstances where human rights abuses are alleged ... Henry Page has brought a claim on behalf of his client, Equatorial Guinea, embodied by its President Teodoro Obiang Nguema Mbasogo, who came to power after deposing and executing his uncle in 1979. Issued in the Queen's Bench Division of the High Court on 30 June 2004, the claim accuses a number of men of attempting to overthrow the president through a well financed coup plot, and seeks redress and damages ... Criticisms have been levelled at the quality of some of the evidence. Allegations of false testimonies and statements obtained by Equatorial Guinea under duress and torture have been made as Page's client pursues the case in the UK; Page strongly refutes the allegations.' Page was reported as saying that his client (Obiang) was 'in fear of his life, and suffered and continues to suffer severe emotional distress.'

The article stated that Page had questioned du Toit in jail. Amnesty International was particularly concerned that, prior to his trial, du Toit's rights to remain silent, and to the presumption of innocence until proven guilty, were 'severely curtailed' by his being exposed to interview by foreign lawyers. 'However, Page denies that Mr du Toit's human rights were breached. Penningtons states: "At no time has Mr Page acted for, or on behalf of, the prosecuting authorities in Equatorial Guinea. The statements taken from Mr du Toit by Mr Page were intended to be (and have been used) to pursue civil claims in England and Guernsey against the European-based architects of the conspiracy. The statements were never intended to be deployed against Mr du Toit in his prosecution in Equatorial Guinea (and were not so used)."' Penningtons said that Page's involvement was all part of a wider inquiry including the dealings of the companies Systems Design Ltd and Logo Ltd.

The *Legal Business* article also included another report over the handling of the trial; this time by the International Bar Association, which also expressed its concerns:

43

Extracts From the trial observation in Equatorial Guinea

An observer for the International Bar Association attended the proceedings in Malabo, Equatorial Guinea, to observe the trial of the 19 alleged mercenaries accused of plotting a coup d'état of the government of President Teodoro Obiang Nguema Mbasogo. The trial commenced on 23 August 2004. In our view, access to counsel and the opportunity to adequately prepare one's defence is a fundamental tenet of the provision of a fair trial. The irregularities described are in breach of the prescribed standards and are procedural breaches which go to the root of the issue as to whether the trial is fair or not. The lack of investigation into allegations of torture is the most troubling feature of this trial. In considering the weight of the evidence against the accused, particularly when reliance is being placed on confessions, there must be certainty that the circumstances of the taking of the statements were free from coercion, torture or ill-treatment. In addition, the issue of whether the accused were tortured goes to the root of whether or not a trial against them is fair or not. In the IBA's view, having regard to international, regional and even the standards laid down in the national laws of Equatorial Guinea, there were sufficient irregularities within the trial that ought to have been taken into account by the tribunal to say that the trial fell short of international fair trial standards . . .

In June 2007, *The Mail on Sunday* was granted exclusive access to Black Beach prison. Du Toit told their reporter: 'It feels like I've been here my whole life. We are locked alone in our cells most of the time while other prisoners go out to the exercise yard and get fresh air. We don't have families living locally to bring us money or food so we can't buy any luxuries, even toothpaste. We cook our own food, mostly just rice, on a gas ring on the landing. That's the only area we are allowed to move around in. We were given grey and white striped prison uniforms but we can't wear them because we are shackled. When Simon Mann arrives he will see what we have gone through for three years and get a taste of it himself. Maybe if he tells them what they want, we will all get out sooner.'

Du Toit later added: 'We thought it might make a difference that he was the one with the evidence, the documents, the paper trail that the government wanted in order to arrest the main financiers of the coup. We felt Simon would want to co-operate and that would help all of us.'

Mann did indeed co-operate fully but while he was well treated in return, conditions for du Toit and the others remained the same. Even after he was sentenced, Mann's special privileges continued for his remaining fourteen months in Black Beach. He was getting high-profile visitors and, unlike du Toit, was not in chains. Du Toit said: 'Simon told me himself that he was getting food brought in daily from a local hotel. We saw platters of food being delivered to his cell Simon was eating luxury food and exercising on his treadmill. He did nothing for me or my men, just looked after himself and paid bribes. We never set eyes on him until the day of that meeting with Jose Olo Obono, the Attorney General, when we heard him discussing payments and then arguing with his wife on the phone.

'After a while, the Attorney General said we could call our wives too. I had had no contact with my wife for two years. Now I was talking to her on the phone, hearing her voice. She said she had written every month for the past six years. I never got her letters. I had written to her too and she had never received a word from me. The Equatorial Guinea government must have been blocking our letters. The six minutes I was allowed on the phone were among the most difficult of my life.'

In November 2009, it was announced that du Toit had been pardonned, together with Simon Mann and three other mercenaries, Sergio Cardoso, Jose Sundays and George Alerson. It was, of course, a desperately-needed release. Recalled du Toit: 'I looked out of my portal and heard Simon shouting over to us, waving madly and asking if we had heard the news. He shouted congratulations. We were all very tearful.'

All the men met up in the courtroom inside the prison. Du Toit said: 'We pledged never to return to Equatorial Guinea, never to engage in plotting against the government, never to disrespect the president. It wasn't hard.'

The same judge who had sentenced them announced they were free and they were taken out to the exercise yard. Du Toit and Mann shook hands. 'His last words to me were that he was going to get everyone, all of them. He said he had paperwork, proof, evidence that would get them locked up,' said du Toit.

Leaving Equatorial Guinea was not without its hitches. Du Toit and the other men were first taken to the airport for a flight to Paris, then Johannesburg and then heard the plans were cancelled. Said du Toit: 'It was chaos. Our luggage was on board and we were about to get on the flight. We heard our government had other plans for us.'

Eventually, they went to a hotel in Malabo where du Toit said: 'For the first time in six years, we had breakfast, lunch and dinner and we watched television.'

At last, back in Johannesburg, police told them they would not be prosecuted there. Du Toit said: 'It was around 2am when I was able to call my wife. She got straight out of bed and drove over to collect me. It was great to be home.'

Du Toit said he had lost five stone in weight during his incarceration at Black Beach. 'Our food was terrible – low-grade rice with dirt and stones in it, fatty meat and everything swimming in palm oil. We spent all day, every day, in chains. We never left our first-floor landing, the maximum risk area, so we never had fresh air. I am a family man. I love my children, all of a sudden not being able to see them, not to receive a letter. In the whole period I was there I received three letters from my wife. I wrote to my daughter every month and she received two letters from me, so it was extremely difficult, another way of torture, keeping us completely locked up from the outside world.'

After his release du Toit told *The Observer*: 'It is difficult to classify the worst period. The first three weeks were very bad; we were treated worse than dogs. But being locked up without any sunshine, solitary confinement, that is the worst of the whole thing. Bad treatment you get over, your body can adapt to it and your mind can take it, but when you sit down on your own 24 hours a day, we are used to being outside; we are outdoors people, so that was extremely difficult.'

It would appear that du Toit greatly underplayed his suffering in Black Beach according to his friend, film-maker James Brabazon. Brabazon supplied this graphic opening to a report in *The Independent* on 8 July 2008:

A man is hanging naked from the ceiling by a meat hook. His feet are bound, but his mouth is open – screaming a confession. He is surrounded by half a dozen soldiers in ragged uniforms whose fists are caked in his blood. Unsatisfied, they taunt him in a language he doesn't understand, as a rifle butt is thrust into his groin. His name is Nick du Toit. He is a South African mercenary, and one of my best friends.

In his final bout of punishment, the air fills with the bitter-sweet tang of roasting meat. It's his own flesh that's burning. Under the flames that spring from the soldiers' cigarette lighters, the fat on the soles of his feet spits and crackles. Opened wide by pain, his eyes gulp in the horror of the concrete cell he's strung up in. Men he has known for years dangle moaning, broken and bleeding. One old friend is already dead. He no longer knows, nor cares, what he is confessing to. After uncounted hours of torture, he is left to the mercy of the rats and the sea. The cell floods at high tide, nearly drowning him, encrusting his wounds with salt.

This is how du Toit began his sentence at Black Beach prison stated Brabazon – who so easily could have been sharing the same punishment as his friend. For du Toit had not only confided in Brabazon about his plan but had asked him to film it. The idea was for Brabazon to be there when the exiled president was flown into Equatorial Guinea 'flanked by black mercenaries, in such a way as to make them look like rebellious local soldiers – and not the remnants of an apartheid-era Special Forces unit.' Added Brabazon: 'This footage – the only television pictures that would exist – would be released to the world's media, buying the new regime time while it took over the institutions of state. In return, I would have exclusive access to film every aspect of the coup for my documentary that I could release once Nick had been paid by the new president.' Brabazon agreed. It was only the death of his grandfather that made him pull out – and saved him from joining du Toit at Black Beach.

Brabazon and du Toit had shared many desperate combat times together. On one occasion, du Toit saved Brabazon's life. They were in rebel-held Liberia where Brabazon was filming a documentary about the conflict. He had hired du Toit as his mercenary body-guard; a decision which proved worthy when the two men were caught in a strafe of machine guns and du Toit dragged Brabazon to safety.

Brabazon had a lucky escape all round. For the plot was rumbled early on and was destined to fail. With news leaking through that a double agent had infiltrated the conspirators, Nick du Toit walked away. Said Brabazon: 'At this point, Nick walked. With Nick off the scene, the tail began to wag the dog. Overall military planning was handed to another operator – who turned out to be an informer for the South African government. In fact, the team of mercenaries had been so thoroughly infiltrated by different intelligence agencies that there were now more spooks organising the plot than genuine conspirators.

'Panicked by the prospect of losing their investments, different financiers began demanding refunds, or selling details of the operation on the commercial intelligence market. Now an open secret, Simon Mann feared the plan (and his future) was doomed. He paid Nick a final visit and persuaded him to sign up again, claiming that the coup's financiers would kill Nick, and his family, if he didn't rejoin. Reluctantly back in the game, Nick fell foul of his own adventure ... My conversations with Nick were tapped by African and Western intelligence services – transcripts of my calls to his satellite phone were shown to me many months later. Everyone had sold out everyone else, and no one seemed able to pose the only question worth asking: what could possibly go wrong?'

Du Toit was himself to admit: 'There was a point about midway through the planning stages when I was on the point of getting out. I told Simon Mann that I didn't think this was viable and we shouldn't continue. All my military experience told me, everything told me, that if the thing has been compromised you can't go ahead with it ... I knew exactly what I was letting myself in for, so the fact that it went wrong, I can't blame anybody. I was there and if everything went well I would have been jumping with joy and I would have had a good business going. So I'm not one of those people who look back and blame everybody else ... I know now that intelligence was zipping from Pretoria to Harare and on to Malabo and that we were always going to be stopped in our tracks.'

Brabazon said: 'When he was sentenced, I broke down in tears. He was my mate when we limped out of the war in Liberia, and he's my mate today. The unpalatable truth is that adversity breeds friendships that transcend moral judgements. In the end, Nick made his choice – which took moral and physical courage – and is paying the price for it.'

Another friend of du Toit, Canadian author and film-maker Robert Young Pelton, wrote how, in January 2006, he attempted to spring du Toit from jail, in the knowledge that the release would have to 'benefit the jailer.' Young Pelton said: 'That usually meant offering a bribe or a swap, or making an appeal for clemency. A jailbreak was a dangerous last resort, but Nick being who he was, his friends kept in touch and were standing by if he needed to be rescued. I said I would try the diplomatic route first. Why me? One of Nick's South African army mates went to EG [Equatorial Guinea] just for a visit and the security police, incredulous at his audacity, sent him directly to jail ... I contacted President Obiang's Paris-based lawyer, Henry Page. His job had been to convict Nick and arrange for the extradition of his co-conspirator, Simon Mann, who had been the alleged mastermind of the coup attempt. I was frank about my friendship with Nick and my goal. From what Nick's friends had told me, I suspected that Nick knew more about the coup's backers than had come out in the trial, and that he had tried to walk away from the plot in its final days. If I got Nick to lay out the whole story, exposing the real planners, would the President reduce his sentence or even pardon him? After all, they were free men; that had to rankle, and cause a few sleepless nights, for Obiang.

'Page seemed open to the discussion so I flew to Paris to meet with him at his elegant 18th century office. The product of the best English public schools, he reminded me of a grown-up Harry Potter. His impeccably polite demeanor disguised his willingness to get his hands dirty – as evidenced by his client list. After a few days, Page had a response for me: Yes, the President will meet with you. A first-class ticket materialized and we flew to Malabo. ... In the waiting room a slight 30 something Lebanese man answered his cell phone incessantly. Potbellied ministers in ill-fitting suits clutched their portfolios and tried not to sweat too much. At last I got the nod to enter the inner sanctum.'

Du Toit's life after the ordeal had its ups and downs. He was refused a visa to visit London by the UK authorities but settled back in South Africa. He said his 'soldier of fortune days were over' and that he regretted his involvement in the coup. 'I am ashamed. It was not a right thing to do. I didn't go there to make lots of money and

49

sit on my own and say, "Hey, I'm a rich man". I did it for my family, to improve their lives. I made the wrong choices, I am very sorry about, for the pain and the grief I brought my family, especially my daughter, who was 10 when I was incarcerated.'

Du Toit insisted not all of his motives in joining in the attempted coup had been about money and said: 'I looked at it in two ways. One was I really do care for Africa because there is a lot of potential in Africa and when it comes to these type of dictators I will help when I can to bring about change. But it was also an opportunity for me to start a new life, financially to get into a proper business and settle down.'

Since his release, du Toit has had no contact with Mann, although he said there are no hard feelings

Now, du Toit says he just wants a quiet life and has realised meddling in other countries' politics can only bring grief. 'I will never go back to the old fighting ways. It is never right to take a course of political action in your own hands by military means. But Africa's history is plagued with wars and battle for power all the time, so it is a place where political views very rarely bring about a change, as it is always the military option and I grew up with that.'

Du Toit said his time in jail had been an opportunity to reflect on his life. 'I have always been an African and even though we really have a lot of problems, we are all pioneers and we should not run away. We should stay and try and change and make the place a better place.

'Even our presence in Equatorial Guinea, in the time that we have been there, getting the whole world's focus on the country, made for a political softening up. It hasn't changed completely, but a lot of the people had been in jail for years without a court case, and after our case a lot of them were taken to court and a lot were freed. So we made a difference. Being called a mercenary – I don't really like it because I am ex-, I am finished with that life.'

Chapter 5

Trials and Retributions

On 10 September 2004, Mann was found guilty of weapons charges by a Zimbabwe magistrate and sentenced to seven years in prison. By this time Mann and his family had already surrendered a plane and several million dollars to Mugabe. The sentence was later reduced to four years. In his absence, he was also found guilty in Equatorial Guinea in November that year, even though his 'trial' would not take place until later.

The next day Tory MP and old friend Henry Bellingham called on the British government to get Mann released and returned to the UK. He said he found it difficult to believe the allegations against his fellow old Etonian and that a British citizen with a distinguished Army career should be helped. 'I have known him for a long time. He has always been an adventurer – but a thoroughly professional one. This just isn't his style, which is one of huge professionalism and making sure he is acting within the law. I find it extraordinary that anyone with his background and experience would go into somewhere like Zimbabwe and buy weapons there. That's asking for everything to go badly wrong. I also say any sentence from a court in Zimbabwe, where the whole legal system has been discredited, is something the British Government must take a close interest in.'

The conditions in Chikurubi jail are harsh. A fellow prisoner of Mann's later told *The First Post* newspaper about the regime. Nathaniel Banda had been sentenced to two years for illegally importing vehicles from South Africa to the Democratic Republic of the Congo via Zimbabwe, where he was caught. He said that

Mann and his fellow conspirators were segregated into one cell 'but conditions for them were just the same as for us.' Banda said that cells meant to house fifteen people often housed forty. 'There is a toilet in the middle. Each cell has a leader and you cannot use the toilet unless you get the okay from the leader. There's never enough water for the toilet and the thing crawls with maggots ... we all had dysentery at some time or other. Food was terrible and it wasn't properly cooked. Mostly *kapenta* (tiny dry fish) in salt water. And mealies, the sort they make for dogs. If you had food sent in from outside like the whites did, it was usually grabbed by the warders. They kept the whites under heavy guard all the time. I used to see Mann when he was taken for a court hearing or when he had a visitor. He would always be manacled, hands and legs. They were scared he would escape somehow ... homosexuality is a big thing in there. Young men are prime targets, and you have to be tough. Many of the men have Aids of course. Work is erratic. I once saw Mann and his people having to clean toilets with no protective gear. Another common job was burying corpses that were rotting, because no-one had claimed them from the city mortuary. If you fall ill there is no treatment. If you protest you are beaten. The only relief is sometimes drugs are smuggled in, usually by wardens.'

It was reported that Mann used his time at Chikurubi to start penning his memoires, scribbling away in Croxley notebooks. A former inmate of his said: 'His only friends were his notebook and pen. He kept writing and writing. He wanted to make sure he finished it before he was extradited. He said he wanted to open a can of worms about who betrayed him.'

On 14 September 2004, the following 'Mercenaries Letter' was published in the *Guardian, Independent* and *Tribune* newspapers.

With regards to the Equatorial Guinea Mercenaries Coup affair involving UK people such as Sir Mark Thatcher and Simon Mann. In light of the fact that over 4 million people (i.e. half of London) have died in violent conflicts in Africa since 1998 (in the last 6 years); over 80% of them being civilians.

The UK Government should urgently:

1. Ratify the UN International Convention against the Recruitment, Use, Financing and Training of Mercenaries as it

would contribute immensely to strengthening of international security; which, as one of the Veto 5 members of the UN Security Council, is one of the UK's prime responsibilities. If the UK feels it cannot ratify the convention in its present form or does not consider it enforceable, they should table changes to it at the UN to make it acceptable.

2. Publish an annual report on the effects and activities of Mercenaries in the world. Special emphasis should be placed on their roles in deadly conflicts; such as in supplying arms to fuel conflicts; the carnage in Africa during the last 6 years; coups and attempted coups.

3. Pass UK legislation controlling Mercenaries. I note from the 2002 UK parliament green paper and debate on private military companies (PMCs). 'The general military view and opinion is that because PMCs are motivated purely by money, the companies involved and their personnel must always be accountable to a nation state and sustainable over a period of time. If PMCs are to be regulated and legislated for, legitimacy and legality should be conveyed in an appropriate and transparent manner. This should involve the UN, EU or a nation state sponsoring PMCs that have no "murky past" and no grounds for being suspected of sponsoring illegal activity.'

Mercenaries seem to represent a lawless, unregulated, un-monitored and generally unreported group who go around the world destroying lives and hindering development. They are a threat to stability, peace and security; a tool for breaking international laws (such as state sovereignty and human rights) and are thus hindering the UK's prime responsibilities in international affairs. The UK government should urgently take effective actions to control this threat.'

Yours Sincerely,
Karl Miller – Secretary – Arms Reduction Coalition

The Arms Reduction Coalition (ARC) is a London-based non-profit, non-government organisation which campaigns for a reduction in the resources spent on arms and the military and for those resources to be diverted to programmes that benefit 'humanity and the earth' such as reducing poverty, sustainable development, 'protecting the vulnerable, systems for peaceful conflict resolutions and maintaining the environment.'

In November 2004, the *Observer* revealed that Britain DID know of the coup plot, with Foreign Minister Jack Straw and Chris Mullin, minister for Africa, personally told of the plans in January that year. It was said they were given dates, details of arm shipments and the names of those involved, but that Straw failed to warn the government of Equatorial Guinea. His admission was made in the House of Commons in answer to a question tabled by the Conservative Shadow Foreign Secretary Michael Ancram. Straw admitted: 'On 29 January this year the Foreign Office received an intelligence report of preparations for a possible coup in Equatorial Guinea. The report was the first intelligence we received. It was not definitive for us to conclude that a coup was likely or inevitable. It was passed on by another government to us on the normal condition that it would not be passed on ... I considered the case and agreed the FCO should approach an individual formerly connected with a British private military company mentioned in the report to 29 January both to attempt to test the veracity of the report and to make clear that the FCO was firmly opposed to an unconstitutional action such as coups d'état. A senior Foreign Office official did so within days. The individual concerned claimed no knowledge of the plans.'

The 'individual' to whom Straw referred was the man described as one of Britain's most notorious mercenaries, and a former business colleague of Mann's – Colonel Tim Spicer – was called into the Foreign Office to discuss the alleged coup more than a month before it was due to take place. Spicer told officials he had no knowledge of any plans for overthrow Obiang. A spokesman for him stated: 'I can confirm that Spicer was called into the Foreign Office in February and was asked about the coup. He told them he knew absolutely nothing about it.'

The disclosure that Straw had seen the intelligence naming a British company in relation to the coup was a stark contrast to the original denial that the British government had no prior knowledge of the plans

The *Observer* reported: 'In his parliamentary answer, Straw attempted to play down the admission that he had received the reports from Smith, claiming it was similar to reports circulating in the Spanish media. Because there were similar rumours the previous year, Straw claimed that the British government was sceptical about its accuracy. He also claimed that his officials could find no definitive evidence of the coup plot. This is hardly credible. Smith's reports give a wealth of information on the coup plans and the individuals involved and South African intelligence must have had knowledge of mercenaries being recruited.

'Everything points to the British, American and also the Spanish governments giving tacit support to a privately funded plot to remove the president of Equatorial Guinea, Teodoro Obiang, and replace him by Severo Moto, a leading opponent of the regime living in exile in Spain. Obiang is said to be in poor health and, whilst the Bush administration and Western regimes are on good terms with this despot, there are fears that if he dies there will be an internecine struggle between possible successors.'

The newspaper added that a close ally of Mann had told its reporters: 'Anyone who knows Simon Mann will know he would never do anything that the British government disapproved of.'

Michael Ancram said: 'It is now clear that Jack Straw's written statement on Equatorial Guinea was inadequate and an ineffective attempt to put an end to the questions being asked about what the British government knew about the planned coup and when they knew it.

And said Ancram: 'Jack Straw's reply raises very significant questions which require answers. Who informed the government, exactly when and what did ministers do with this information?'

Ancram had tabled several further parliamentary questions about exactly what Britain knew about the intended coup. His concerns were echoed by Menzies Campbell, the Liberal Democrats' foreign affairs spokesman, who said: 'This reply characteristically raises more questions than it answers. Not only do we need to know what steps did the government take to warn the government of Equatorial Guinea, but what steps they took to ensure that British citizens did not become involved.'

The Foreign Office refused to explain the background to Straw's answer arguing that it was 'sub judice'. Meanwhile, the government of Equatorial Guinea was threatening to take Straw to the International Court of Justice in The Hague for his lack of action. The country's lawyers claimed that under international conventions,

Straw had had a legal obligation to pass on any warning about a coup and said it was 'deeply suspicious' that no investigation was being carried out into the suspects behind the plot, adding, 'It is difficult to imagine a more serious crime than planning to murder the leader of a sovereign country, along with his senior officers. The conspiracy was hatched in London.'

On 17 April 2005, *The Observer* reported on the plight of the eleven foreign nationals, including Nick du Toit who were languishing in Equatorial Guinea's Black Beach prison. It said that according to Amnesty International, conditions inside the prison had deteriorated so seriously in the last six weeks that at least seventy prisoners were at imminent risk of starvation. 'The majority of these detainees are South African nationals. Their alleged activities and arrests have been linked to the arrest of 64 other suspected mercenaries in Zimbabwe on 7 March 2004. They also include dozens of Equatorial Guinean political detainees arrested in 2004 who are being held without charge or trial.

'According to Amnesty International, provision of food by the authorities has been reduced from a cup of rice daily in December 2004 to one or two bread rolls a day, and since the end of February 2005 provision of any prison food has been sporadic, with prisoners reportedly going for up to six days at a time without any food.

'Prisoners and detainees are now dependent on food handed to prison guards by families. This means that the 11 foreign nationals and dozens of Equatorial Guinean political detainees arrested on the mainland are particularly at risk of starvation because they do not have families in Malabo to support them.

'Many of those detained at Black Beach prison are already extremely weak because of the torture or ill-treatment they have suffered and because of chronic illnesses for which they have not received adequate medical treatment.

'All those imprisoned are kept inside their cells 24 hours a day and the foreign nationals are also kept with their hands and legs cuffed at all times. The authorities have blocked almost all contact with families, lawyers and consular officials'.

Political exile, Weja Chicampo, told how he spent two years at Black Beach prison where he was tortured, threatened with death and kept in a cell without light with up to fifteen other inmates. He was arrested at gunpoint in 2004 and accused of 'distributing propaganda'. When he regained consciousness he was in jail. Chicampo said that now even Mann's military training could not save him from madness, if not death, were he to be similarly incarcerated. 'If they keep him in solitary confinement, as they do for the most serious prisoners, then he could lose his mind even if he is a tough man. When I was there, one man lost the ability to speak, he had been alone for so long. I was in a small cell with ten other men in the dark. It was hot, and it smelt very bad as they would not let us out to go to the toilet. I had a badly injured arm, shoulder and hip. But I got no medical attention. They fed us on two small pieces of bread every two days and a cup of water. They kept me for two months with no contact with the outside world. Then they brought me before a judge and accused me of illicit association. I was simply a member of a group calling for the rights of a minority.' Chicampo was sent back to prison without trial, having been refused contact with a lawyer or his family, and was denied visits or medical attention. He was badly beaten and left without water so he had to drink his own urine. He was accused of being connected with the coup plotters, whom he did not know. But hardest to bear was the psychological torture. He said: 'They tell you they are going to kill you or you are going to die. Or worse, you hear other prisoners getting tortured, their screams in the night. It is always in the night.' (After pressure from foreign governments and organisations including Amnesty International, he was eventually released and expelled from the country in 2006.)

Concern for du Toit and the others inside Black Beach prison increased following the death that year of German national, Gerhard Eugen Nershz, who was arrested in connection with the coup plot. He died on 17 March after what authorities described as 'cerebral malaria with complications' – though he was also said to have died of a heart attack. Nershz was taken to hospital from the prison some hours before his death and people who saw him reported that he appeared to have severe injuries caused by torture on his hands and feet. Abel Augusto who was detained with Nershz said he had died from trauma following torture after he had 'enraged the interrogators because when they hit him he never said a word.' This apparently provoked more severe battering before Nershz was dumped back in his cell. It was said that prisoners called for medical help for him but were ignored. 'No one has seen the body, so no one is in a position to say,' said Amnesty International spokesperson Marise Castro. Another detainee, 'Bones' Boonzaaier, who was already ill before he was arrested, was denied any medical treatment at least until a South African delegation met the detainees on 18 March.

The fate of inmates at Black Beach has always given cause for concern. The United Nations, the American State Department as well as Amnesty, have all drawn attention to the 'disappearance' of three members of the Equatorial Guinea armed forces and a civilian. All four were later found guilty of planning a coup. In September 2002, prisoner Juan Asumu Sima died shortly after being found guilty of another coup attempt. During the trial Sima needed help to stand and reportedly had scars on his legs and arms, consistent with accounts that he was severely tortured in detention. He repeatedly asked for medical assistance but was refused. Some months later, Felipe Ondo Obiang, head of one of the opposition parties to the President and accused of being involved in another coup attempt, also vanished. (He had already been sentenced to twenty years in Black Beach.) There was speculation that he had been abducted, and he has not been seen since. One inmate had his hands whipped so badly he was unable to sign a confession – which had been invented. Jaws of prisoners have been broken and forearms snapped in half.

At least thirteen other co-accused remain in Black Beach – most, if not all, were severely tortured at the time of their arrest, according to Amnesty, which added that they were. But even basic human rights towards Black Beach prisoners are not adhered to.

Amnesty International UK campaigns director Stephen Bowen said: 'Such near starvation, lack of medical attention and appalling prison conditions are nothing short of a slow, lingering death sentence for these prisoners. The authorities must provide food and medicine immediately and grant access to international monitors. Unless immediate action is taken many of those detained at Black Beach prison will die.'

In April 2005, the tax haven of Guernsey came under the spotlight when it faced the dilemma of whether it should release bank records. Not just any bank records of course, but those relating to the failed coup. British lawyers acting for Equatorial Guinea had requested an order from Guernsey's La Court Ordinaire for records that should reveal who bankrolled the £3m failed coup. They wanted to see bank accounts and safe deposit boxes belonging to two companies owned by Simon Mann, which are held at the Royal Bank of Scotland International on Guernsey. The high-profile case brought unwelcome media attention to the discreet Channel Island. After decades of being seen as a haven for money laundering and tax evasion, Guernsey had been attempting to improve its international image in the past few years. 'It is clear that Guernsey is not and cannot be a safe haven for criminals and fraudsters. We have a framework that stands up to international scrutiny,' said the islands Deputy Bailiff Geoffrey Rowland. Alex Yearsley of the campaigning group Global Witness said: 'This is the perfect opportunity for the regulatory and financial authorities in Guernsey to show the world at large that they are transparent and accountable and to dispel the widely held view that their banking and financial laws hamper serious investigations by the relevant authorities.' Mann's lawyers challenged the court application. In the end, the Court of Appeal in Guernsey ruled that details of individuals paying money into accounts on the island should not be turned over to Obiang's lawyers.

In June, Obiang pardoned six Armenians who had been amongst those convicted of being involved in the coup attempt. This followed intense lobbying by the Armenian government and campaigners.

On 30 June 2006, BBC Two screened *Coup!* a satirical look at a 'tale of audacity, incompetence and betrayal' – Mann's thwarted coup attempt. Written by satirist John Fortune and starring Jared Harris as Mann, the film was described as dealing with 'greed, money and how countries rich in oil will always become the centre of the world's attention' – whether wanted or not. It exposes the arrogance of well-connected old Etonians like Mann, founder of mercenary firm Executive Outcomes. Executive Producer Jess Pope said: 'This is the story of a plot of astonishing audacity. A small coterie of well-connected, white, middle-class Englishmen were arrogant to believe that they could storm in and plunder the rights to the oil reserves of a minor African dictatorship in a "get rich quick" scheme to shore up their own private pensions. What they hadn't reckoned on was the coming of age of the new, anti-mercenary South Africa.'

On 23 February 2007, the charges against Mann and the other alleged conspirators were dropped in South Africa. Magistrate Peel

Johnson, sitting in the Pretoria Regional Court, threw the case out after a number of state witnesses claimed the attempted coup was sanctioned by the South African, British, Spanish and US governments. The magistrate ruled there was credible evidence by the state's witnesses that the South African government sanctioned the coup, or that the accused were under the impression that it was sanctioned. Johnson found that the state had not proved its case against the men, and that while the actions of the men were unlawful, he could not find by 'any stretch of the imagination' that they had knowingly contravened the Regulation of Foreign Military Assistance Act. The director general of the South African secret service, Hilton Dennis, admitted that he knew of the plot but did not sanction it. He allowed the men to fly out of South Africa because 'There are many ways to kill a cat. We chose this route and succeeded in preventing the coup.'

Mann remained in Zimbabwe where he was convicted of charges from the plot. On 2 May 2007, Magistrate Omega Mugambate ruled that Mann should be extradited to Equatorial Guinea to face charges with the promise he would not face the death sentence. She declared: 'The extradition application is not prohibited in terms of the law. [The] respondent did not prove charges of torture while [the] applicant provided a prima facie case against respondent. It is hereby ordered that respondent be extradited to Equatorial Guinea.'

Mann's lawyer Jonathan Samkange insisted that Mann had been tortured saying: 'I have requested the court to investigate the findings that Mann had been tortured in the run-up to the extradition hearings to force a pre-determined outcome to the process ... My client was severely tortured by members of the military intelligence and Central Intelligence Organisation operatives in prison. The prison authorities have not denied that Mann was tortured during unscheduled visits by state security agents. Simon Mann has already been tortured here in prison and we will not have him extradited to Equatorial Guinea for further torture. He has been tortured at the request of a country applying to have him tried under its jurisdiction.'

Chapter 6

Mishaps of a Mummy's Boy

On 24 August 2004, Mark Thatcher was arrested at his Cape Town home in connection with the aborted coup. His arrest was particularly sensational because of his famous long-serving Prime Minister mother. It was by no means the first time he had made the news – or caused his mother anxiety. But it was certainly the most dramatic. His family background, colourful and often controversial private and business lives, make him the perfect addition to the Equatorial Guinea fiasco. Something of a 'mummy's boy' (and much weaker than his twin sister Carol) Mark wasted no time in taking advantage of being the son of a Prime Minister. As soon as his mother came to power in 1979 he demanded bodyguards of his own – their cost a fudged issue by Mrs Thatcher when she was tackled by the Home Office following questions by concerned MPs. On the back of his mother's election as Prime Minister, too, Thatcher set up his own company, international consultancy Monteagle Marketing, did some modelling, advertised swimwear in America which was rewarded with a $40,000 fee and received $50,000 for promoting whisky in Japan. There was also the lucrative deal with a Japanese textile firm – something which raised eyebrows when his mother was urging everyone to 'buy British'. The *Financial Times* described Thatcher as a 'sort of Harrovian Arthur Daley with a famous mum.' Thatcher was to later to be viewed as a serious liability in Downing Street, although no one dared raise the subject with his mother who had a blind spot about her son. When Bernard Ingham, Mrs Thatcher's plain-speaking press secretary, was asked how her son could best help in an upcoming re-election campaign, he famously replied: 'Leave the country.'

In 1982, Thatcher, his French co-driver Anne-Charlotte Verney and their mechanic, known only as 'Jackie', went missing for six days in the Sahara Desert while competing in the Paris-Dakar rally. As Britain's Prime Minister, Mark's mother was already facing challenges enough for it was the year of the Falklands War, a conflict which began in April that year and ended in June.

It was on 9 January that the rally trio became separated from a convoy of vehicles after they stopped to make repairs to both broken trailing arm-links and broken rear axle on their white Peugeot 504. The Sahara is not a good place to be lost in. Known as 'The Great Desert', it is the world's largest hot desert, its 9,400,000 square kilometres (3,630,000 square miles) covering most of North Africa and almost equalling Europe or the USA. The group's disappearance was not reported until 12 January when a massive search was launched involving spotter planes and helicopters and rescuers from four countries. 'The Boss' as Thatcher called his mother, had used her influence to call the ambassador in Algiers. A C-130 Hercules search plane from the Algerian military eventually spotted their car some 50km off course on 14 January. They were tired, hungry and thirsty (eking out their five-litre water supply to two polystyrene cups each a day and nibbling on dried food) but unharmed.

Their plight made big news, with the press finding it hard to disguise its cynicism about what they perceived as Thatcher's attempt to undertake a challenge he was not up to. Thatcher himself had to agree. He spoke about his ordeal after flying back home in an Algerian presidential plane with his father Denis who had gone out to join the hunt. Thatcher admitted to the *Guardian:* 'I did absolutely no preparation. Nothing. I did half a day's testing and the day after that we were driving out of the Place de la Concorde in Paris. I was thinking, "OK, I wonder how this is going to go?" I soon found out ... Unfortunately the Peugeot 504 was the very worst car to do the trip in. It was a very long-wheelbase car, and what you need is a short-wheelbase car because of all the bumps. I remember thinking, two days before we stopped, that this could all go very badly wrong.' Upon Thatcher's safe return, his stoic mother commented: 'It's all right now and life to me looks totally different personally from what it did two days ago. It puts your other personal worries into perspective.' The whole episode provoked recall of Mark's nickname 'Thickie' during his days at Harrow School. After leaving Harrow in 1971, he failed his accountancy exams three times and one of his short-term jobs was with Touche Ross, a City of London firm of Chartered Accountants. In fact Thatcher went through a series of jobs, each lasting about a year. He dabbled in the Hong Kong business world and built up a network of associates from the Middle and Far East and the motor-racing world.

In 1977, Thatcher set up Mark Thatcher Racing, a car-racing company which became best with financial problems.

In 1981, Thatcher was secretly paid commission by construction firm Cementation for the building of a new university in Oman. It was a contract his mother had personally lobbied the sultan of Oman for during a visit. Files released some years later showed that Ivor Lucas, ambassador to Oman at the time, had sent a note to Whitehall saying he believed the Prime Minister's son was associated with the firm and that the Sultan had promised her the contract. He added: 'it is a little surprising that this decision should have been taken at such an early stage and that Cementation should have scooped the jackpot ... they were by no means the first in the field.' Cementation in turn claimed in a letter that the Prime Minister had promised it preferential government finance terms. Despite there being no money available for the project, all relevant government departments were urged to make it happen and Mrs Thatcher made her enthusiasm for it apparent. She always denied a conflict of interests and said she had just been 'Batting for Britain'. Thatcher severed his links with Cementation and left his Downing Street flat.

Three years later, the *Observer* newspaper exposed the background to the Oman deal. Questions were raised in the House of Commons, public rows ensued and Mark Thatcher was dispatched to America, presumably until the heat died down. He complained he was 'not appreciated'. All was not lost, however, as he was leaving to take up a £45,000 deal to promote Lotus and British Car Auctions.

But the 'mummy's boy' still had his mummy worrying about him again. She did not feel he was safe there, having allowed the USA to use British bases to bomb Libya. Mrs Thatcher wrote a memo to Nigel Wicks, her principal private secretary: 'I fear he may be a priority target. I thought the security people over there would automatically [this word was double-underlined] think of giving him special protection, but nothing has happened.' The FBI complained about the resources needed to give Mark Thatcher 24-hour protection and he eventually agreed to move into his own tight-security home. His father suggested Mark might like to pay for any security measures out of his own pocket, for fear of a backlash if it was known taxpayers' money was used. It was clear who wore the trousers in the Thatcher household. She drew the line at public money being used on the bullet-proof windows her son demanded, but she still sent out the order that taxpayers should cough up £31,000 for an alarm system and 'panic room'. (He later had stakes in his own burglar alarm company!) One wonders just who Mark Thatcher was afraid of. That same year, 1984, a confidential briefing prepared for George Shultz, then US Secretary of State, had this to say about Mark Thatcher's business acumen: 'Most of his business dealings were predicated on the belief that he had only one asset – with a limited life span – his link to the British prime minister'

In 1986, there was the controversial allegation that Thatcher had visited Brunei with the businessman and Harrod's owner Mohamed Al Fayed resulting in rival Harrod's would-be purchaser Tiny Rowland, chief executive of company Lonrho, owner of the *Observer*, being thwarted in his bid. The allegations claimed Al Fayed was backed by Mrs Thatcher's government and were denied by all parties involved.

It was during his time in America that Thatcher met and married Dallas socialite Diane Burgdorf, daughter of a Texas millionaire car dealer. The wedding in February 1987 was organised by the Downing Street press office. Shortly afterwards, Dallas computer firm EDS expressed a desire to put Thatcher on its payroll. Despite the company lobbying for government contracts and being under investigation for not securing UK work permits for its staff, 'My Mummy the Prime Minister' agreed. Then followed yet more press furore.

Around this time, it was rumoured that Thatcher received as much as £12m for helping with Britain's record arms deal sale to Saudi Arabia. Yet again, his mother played a big part in encouraging the contract to be offered to British defence firms. The deal – '*Al Yamamah*' – followed on from Thatcher's friendships within the arms business; friendships he had enjoyed for some years. One, businessman Wafic Said, was involved in the arms deal. He gave Thatcher a Rolex watch. It was later claimed by Adnan Khashoggi, the international arms dealer, that 'Wafic realised Thatcher's usefulness and that whenever he needed a question answered Thatcher would go directly to his mother for the answer.' Thatcher always denied receiving any money. But one man, Howard Teicher, a Middle East expert on Ronald Reagan's National Security Council in the 1980s, later told *The Independent on Sunday* newspaper: 'I read of Mark Thatcher's involvement in this arms deal in dispatches from our embassy in Saudi Arabia, from intelligence reports that were gleaned in Saudi Arabia and Europe and in diplomatic dispatches from other European capitals. I considered these dispatches totally reliable, totally accurate. I did not think that people would loosely accuse the son of the Prime Minister of being involved in such a transaction unless they were certain it was the case, and the fact that I saw his name appear in a number of different sourced documents convinced me of the authenticity of at least the basic involvement on Mark Thatcher's part. He was clearly playing some kind of role to help facilitate the completion of a transaction between the two governments.'

In the autumn of 1989, shortly after the birth of their first child Michael, Diane and Mark took a ten-day break at the Eden Roc hotel in Antibes, in the south of France. There they became acquainted with the three daughters of millionaire property developer Terence Clemence. One, Sarah-Jane, caught Thatcher's eye. After the trip Diane returned to Dallas and Thatcher flew to Paris on a business trip. Diane later discovered her husband had been spending time with Sarah-Jane. She confronted them both with Thatcher promising never to see the other woman again. It was a promise he was not to keep.

In November 1992, concerns were raised in the House of Commons that during the 1980–88 war between Iraq and Iran the British Government had actively encouraged the sale of weapons to Iraq, and possibly Iran, in spite of a declared veto on doing so; that British banks were actively supporting this effort and had highly-trained teams helping them do so; and that people close to the British Government, including possibly the former Prime Minister Margaret Thatcher's son Mark, were making large sums of money from the arms trade. It was further alleged that Thatcher was a friend of Carlos Cardoen, a Chilean arms manufacturer responsible for supplying Saddam Hussein with a variety of military equipment including chemical weapons technology. Shortly afterwards Thatcher made a rare reply to parliamentary accusations aimed at him about his deals. He said: 'They have nothing on me. This is the thanks I get for being a good British businessman.'

Other issues raised in the House of Commons included allegations Thatcher had promoted the sale of heavy artillery to Saudi Arabia at a time when Britain had an embargo on the country and that he had offered to act as middleman for the South African state arms manufacturer Armscor in a deal said to be worth more than £3m.

Thatcher and his wife moved to South Africa with their children Michael and Amanda in 1995. One of their acquaintances in their dinner party circle was neighbour Simon Mann

In 2000, Thatcher tried to do business with Equatorial Guinea through a company called *Cogito*, which he had set up to provide security advice and intelligence to multi-national companies in Africa. *Cogito* offered the president Obiang Nguema Mbasogo a £134,000 contract to gather intelligence on his opponents and draw up threat assessments. Thatcher hoped it would lead to securing valuable oil concessions, but in the end Obiang rejected the offer. Was this was prompted Thatcher's dangerous involvement with the country four years later?

Early in the morning on 25 August 2004, police swooped on Thatcher's Constantia mansion with a search warrant. Six hours later, and after his computers, mobile phones and personal items were seized, he was driven away. He appeared in court that afternoon charged with contravening Sections Two and Three of the Foreign Military Assistance Act 1998, which bans South African residents from taking part in any foreign military activity. The charges related to 'possible funding and logistical assistance in relation to [an] attempted coup in Equatorial Guinea. Court papers showed that the 'Scorpion' police squad had waited five days before getting a warrant for Thatcher's arrest, arriving on his doorstep the very same day that British Foreign Secretary Jack Straw was in South Africa for bilateral talks on economic issues. His visit was knocked off the front pages by Thatcher's arrest. This led to talk amongst Thatcher's friends that the arrest was politically motivated (Margaret Thatcher was no friend to the now ruling African National

Congress during the apartheid era and once referred to Nelson Mandela as a terrorist).

Thatcher was released on bail of £167,000 – paid by his mother of course – and warned not to leave the Cape Town area. He was ordered to surrender his passport and to check in each day with police officials. He was also banned from going near an airport because the authorities believed he was preparing to flee South Africa for Dallas with his wife and children. (Thatcher had sold four luxury SUV cars, had made approaches about selling his £3m mansion and had apparently had his bags packed when he was arrested.) He was later bailed to London to live with his mother while Diane and the children moved to Dallas without him.

The arrest of the son of Lady Thatcher made headlines around the world. Despite his title, 51-year-old Thatcher was to receive no special treatment by his accusers (he is entitled to be called 'Sir' following his mother's peerage as a baroness in 1992 and, following the death of his father Sir Denis in 2003, inherited the Thatcher baronetcy. It was former Prime Minister John Major who awarded Denis Thatcher his baronetcy. Major later admitted he had been reluctant to award the title but had been lobbied by 'influential figures').

On 24 November 2004, the Cape Town High Court upheld a subpoena from the South African Justice Ministry that required Thatcher to answer under oath questions from Equatorial Guinean authorities regarding the alleged coup attempt. He was due to face questioning on 25 November 2004, regarding offences under the South African Foreign Military Assistance Act but the proceedings were later postponed until 8 April 2005.

In the weeks preceding the hearing, rumours flew around as to just what the authorities had on Thatcher. Piet van der Merwe who spearheaded his arrest said that his computer files contained incriminating evidence. Another source said that the main evidence lay in a statement given by one of Thatcher's closest friends. Commented police spokesman Sipho Ngwema: 'We would not have arrested him if we did not think we had a case.' Obiang himself declared Thatcher to be a 'dirty player. He lived his life getting involved in all sorts of dubious deals. He was a friend of Simon Mann and expected huge benefits. Mark Thatcher quickly jumped on the boat and became part and parcel of this plot.'

Thatcher protested his innocence and issued a statement through his friend and unofficial spokesman, public relations guru Lord Timothy Bell – best known for his advisory role in Margaret Thatcher's three successful general election campaigns. On Thatcher's behalf, Lord Bell declared: 'I have no involvement in any alleged coup in Equatorial Guinea and I reject totally all suggestions to the contrary.'

But damning details emerged and more and more people concluded Thatcher was lying to save his skin. Sir Bernard Ingham told *The Times* he thought it was 'very difficult to believe' Thatcher did not know what was going on, adding: 'He's not the brightest spark but by God he knows how to make money. The plain fact is, he's a barrow boy.'

It was revealed that in November 2003, Mann and Thatcher had had several meetings in London to discuss 'transport ventures' in West Africa. Thatcher would insist that he was never told about the coup, but admitted agreeing to finance the chartering of an air-ambulance helicopter for one of Mann's 'ventures'. He did admit his suspicions later that it might be used for 'mercenary activities'. There was time for Thatcher to pull out of any involvement, but he didn't. That December, the newly widowed Lady Thatcher flew to Cape Town to spend Christmas with her son, daughter-in-law and two grandchildren, Michael, then aged fourteen, and Amanda, ten. The Thatchers held their traditional pre-Christmas drinks party around the swimming pool in the garden on 22 December. Among the guests were Simon Mann and Crause Steyl, the pilot who had worked for him on previous operations. The two had first met when Mann established Executive Outcomes and won the contract to run military operations in support of the Angolan government's operations against the Unita rebels. Steyl had also worked on several other private military operations such as the Executive Outcomes contract in Sierra Leone.

On 12 January 2004, Mann wrote a memo outlining the potential risks in the operation that appeared to directly implicate Thatcher. Mann wrote: 'If MT's involvement is known, the rest of us and the project is likely to be screwed – as a side-issue to people screwing him ... Ensure doesn't happen.' Four days later, Thatcher signed an agreement with Crause Steyl committing him to a maximum investment of $500,000 in an air ambulance company

Simon Mann later confirmed whilst in jail that Thatcher was 'part of the team.' He said that Thatcher was 'not just an investor; he came completely on board and became a part of the management team.' Mann then spoke in court about taking Thatcher to the London home of a businessman (who was alleged by the government of Equatorial Guinea to have been the main financier of the attempted coup). Telephone records later obtained by a private detective hired by Henry Page, a Paris-based lawyer representing the government of Equatorial Guinea, showed that Thatcher and Mann spoke very often in the days immediately before the coup. Mr Page said: 'Of course we don't know what was said; only that Mark Thatcher's number appears on the record of Simon Mann's calls with increasing frequency.' It was claimed that the records also showed four calls between the businessman and disgraced MP Jeffrey Archer and five calls to Thatcher from Wales.

Other claims were equally explosive. It was said that Thatcher financed the $350,000 purchase of a small plane that would be used to transport the proposed provisional president Severo Moto from his opposition exile in Spain to Malabo via the Canary Islands. Moto is the most notable opposition politician in Equatorial Guinea and leader of the country's Progress Party. From Spain, he established a government in exile greatly incurring the wrath of Teodoro Obiang.

Crause Steyl, one of the pilots picked to fly the coup leaders in a chartered King 200 twin turbo prop aircraft, registered ZS-NBJ from Us Dodson Aviation, later turned prosecution witness in South Africa and said: 'I met Mark [Thatcher] three or four times. He was a partner in the venture. He put in about $250,000. The money was wired to my company account in various installments. The helicopters cost about $600 an hour plus $5,000 each for the pilots and $10,000 a month for special insurance.' Steyl decided to co-operate with the prosecution side because of fears over his brother Neil who had helped pilot the Boeing 727 and was now languishing in Chikurubi prison on a fourteen month sentence. Like Thatcher, he too later had to face charges in South Africa under the Regulations of Foreign Military Assistance Act. According to the court brief, Crause Steyl felt bad about his brother's fate because 'it was he who promised his brother $1m to fly the Boeing 727. Neil had a good job flying an Indian-based tycoon, now he's in Chikurubi.'

On 28 August 2004, the *Observer* reported how Crause Steyl had turned 'state witness' and was alleged to have given 'dramatic new evidence to South African police who were investigating Mark Thatcher's role.' It said Steyl was believed to have handed over details of Thatcher's investment in an aviation firm that had contracts with Simon Mann, and added: 'Steyl's evidence could be highly damaging to Thatcher, who faces 15 years in jail after being charged last week with helping to finance the mercenary plot to topple the President. The government of Equatorial Guinea is requesting an interview with Thatcher in South Africa and is hoping to have him extradited to face trial there. Thatcher's defence team in Cape Town – which insists he is innocent of all charges – believes Steyl is emerging as central to the prosecution and say they have been told to stay away from him. The lawyers suspect that Steyl has given the South African police a detailed affidavit containing several statements.' Steyl was unavailable for comment.

Steyl dismissed Thatcher's claim that he believed he was paying for an air ambulance saying: 'He knew what was going on. I only knew him in the context of the Equatorial Guinea business. I didn't know him before and I haven't met him since.' Others were more convinced of Thatcher's involvement. 'We allege he is one of the financiers of the coup to overthrow the government of Equatorial Guinea and we have received credible evidence that he has assisted financially in that regard. Anyone who is using this country as a springboard for violence and disorder, we are going to deal with those persons quite strongly.' said Sipho Ngwema, a spokesman for the elite Scorpions investigative unit of the South African police.

Another man involved in the coup attempt, mercenary veteran Nick du Toit, also spoke of Thatcher's part. He told friend, film maker and author James Brabazon: 'I knew he [Mann] was working with Mark Thatcher and others who had British government connections, so yes, I believed it ... the Thatcher name was not a big one to me because his mother was the prime minister; not him, so he didn't impress me much, but he was a connection of Simon and through Simon I trusted him.'

Mark Hollingsworth, co-author of *Thatcher's Fortunes: The Life and Times of Mark Thatcher*, said: 'Mark could not resist being involved. He attended planning meetings at Simon Mann's house, knew exactly what was going on and was looking for a slice of the action.

The notion that he would invest $500,000 and not know what it was used for is risible. He hero-worshipped Mann and loved the secret world of soldiers of fortune, spies and high-risk shady business deals in oil-trading and gunrunning.'

Yet when Mann wrote to Thatcher from jail asking for his help in securing his release – something which depended more on available money than a fair trial – Thatcher ignored him. The *Daily Mail* pointed out how Thatcher had done deals with Mugabe's regime in Zimbabwe and had often claimed to have some clout with the country's leader. The paper added: 'But Sir Mark – famous for translating his three Harrovian O-levels and the helpfulness of his surname into a successful life as a trader in commodities (and with connections that have never been entirely explained) – allegedly declined to help and Mann languished in prison.'

Nick Morgan, the ex-guardsman suspected of blowing the whistle on the attempted coup, said Thatcher had not known about the coup plot. 'I can tell you that Mark was not directly involved,' he said. 'The allegations are circumstantial, resulting from his friendship with Mann and his unwise contractual agreement with Steyl ... I had lunch with someone [I thought was involved] to try to stop him from going, and I said, "I hope you weren't stupid enough to get Mark involved. You know that whatever he does attracts media and intelligence."' Morgan added that the mystery person promised he had not involved Thatcher in his plans, and Morgan said he believes him. 'If I'd thought Mark was anywhere near this thing I'd have handcuffed him to an aircraft and flown him out of the country.'

But leaked confidential legal documents stated: 'The accused began to doubt Mann's true intentions and suspected that Mann might be planning to become involved in mercenary activity in the West African region. Despite his misgivings, the accused decided to invest money in the charter of the helicopter. In fact, Mann did intend to use the helicopter in mercenary activity.' A source in the South African investigation team said: 'Thatcher has given us a lot of evidence that we need to consider before we make our next move.'

While still in South Africa, Thatcher had a meeting arranged by Lord Tim Bell and Bell's associate Abel Haddon, with Vicky Ward, a reporter from *Vanity Fair* but 'at Thatcher's insistence, Haddon stipulated that there were to be no questions about the court hearing scheduled for late November concerning Thatcher's possible involvement in funding an alleged multi-million-dollar failed coup attempt in the oil-rich dictatorship of Equatorial Guinea, a tiny former Spanish colony on the west coast of Africa.' The *Vanity Fair* article said that 'currently Thatcher really is a figure in exile. He used to receive dozens of e-mails a day; now it's down to three. His phone calls and e-mails are monitored. "I will never be able to do business again," he says. He adds that on the day of his arrest there were 18,500 Google mentions about it. "Who will want to deal with me after that?" he asks with a shrug."Furious? Yes, I think you can let me say on the record that being arrested is likely to infuriate anyone." This time there is a flash of passion in his eye.'

Thatcher said he was grateful his father was not still alive to see him in his predicament and that he spoke to his mother on the phone twice a week. 'He is like his mother in that he doesn't show emotion,' said Tim Bell. 'He's used to people insulting him and abusing him and accusing him of things.' Some of Thatcher's friends said 'born guilty.' Commented Thatcher: 'I've never heard that before but I just feel in this particular case like a corpse that's going down the Colorado River and there's nothing I can do about it.'

While publicly denying any significant role, in January 2005 Thatcher pleaded guilty in South Africa – after a plea bargain – to 'unwittingly' abetting the coup, because he had provided an aircraft without questioning its use. He said he believed the money was to be used for 'humanitarian purposes.' Thatcher was fined 3m rand (£266,000), given a suspended four-year jail term, and ordered to leave South Africa. As part of the deal, he was required to co-operate with the ongoing investigation. In fact Thatcher had already had talks with the South African Intelligence Service – possibly because they threatened to extradite him to Equatorial Guinea if he did not co-operate. There were some who felt Thatcher had committed an act of betrayal to save his own skin. A source close to Mann said: 'After Simon has gone out of his way to portray Mark as whiter than white, this is a terrible betrayal. While Simon is dying in one of Africa's worst prisons, Thatcher is free to roam the globe after buying his way out of trouble. He might well have sentenced Simon to death.' As he left the court in Cape Town, Thatcher justified his willingness to co-operate saying: 'There is no price too high for me to pay to be reunited with my family. I am sure all of you who are husbands and fathers will understand that'. Across the street, a poster reading 'Save me mummy' hung from a window.

Thatcher returned to South Africa in February to answer further questions about his involvement with the coup. He was asked whether he knew a number of people alleged to have been involved in the plot to overthrow Teodoro Obiang Nguema, and he said he knew most of them, but only socially. Thatcher was also asked as well about his relationship with Simon Mann and why Mann had claimed he had agreed to provide funds for the coup attempt. Thatcher replied: 'I'm not aware that Mr Mann made any such claims and if he did, I can't think of a reason why he should have done.'

On leaving the court, Thatcher told reporters: 'It is a mystery to me why I should give evidence in a trial that ended four months ago.

'However, I'm very happy to have had the opportunity to do so, and to do so under oath, because as you have observed from my answers to the questions it is patently clear that I had nothing to do with financing any coup in Equatorial Guinea.'

That same month there were calls for Thatcher to be stripped of his hereditary title. Tony Wright, Labour chairman of the Commons Public Administration Committee, which had investigated the honours system, said: 'If we give honours for honours, we should remove them for dishonours.' He was supported by Sir Menzies Campbell, Liberal Democrat foreign affairs spokesman: 'The award of a hereditary title to Denis Thatcher was deeply controversial at the time. The reservations expressed then are more than justified by the fact that Mark Thatcher has pleaded guilty to a serious criminal offence which could well have profoundly damaging consequences for British interests abroad.'

In June 2006, BBC 2 screened *Coup!* a satirical look at the aborted coup and Thatcher's part in it. Commented director Simon Cellan Jones: 'With all these scenes of planes and storming of airports, it was easy to get wrapped up in the adventure of it all. We had to remind ourselves that we had to keep things serious; amid the mockery of these deeply incompetent marauders, we needed some lasting bite. To be blunt, men like Mark Thatcher don't need our help to look comical.' The *Observer*'s Phil Hogan reviewed the film: 'Mark Thatcher's walk-on part in a botched African coup a couple of years ago was more a gift to lovers of satire than seasoned watchers of international affairs. But though the story – a British-led mercenary plot to seize the squalid but oil-rich state of Equatorial Guinea – lapsed occasionally into farce, comedy was never quite going to do it justice. Dramatising the doomed excursion in *Coup!*, John Fortune (of TV's *Bird and Fortune*) seemed only grudgingly to acknowledge this, preferring to portray "the boy Mark" in the colours of panto-mime villain than take on the admittedly knotty problem of teasing out a possible second dimension to his character. Thatcher's fellow "entrepreneurs" were equally preposterous – blazery, slack-jawed, Old Etonian golf-botherers of the sort you might expect to see lampooned on stage by Fortune himself; the sort of people who call money "wonga". It was only a matter of time before someone from the impersonation agency was called up to play a frail Lady T (Caroline Blakiston) trying to flag down passing party guests in an effort to secure a large Scotch. "Very little water," she whispered, meaning none.'

Thatcher's life began to fall apart after his conviction. His wife, Diane, returned to the US with the children, and on 19 September 2005 the couple announced their intention to divorce. There had been other infidelities by Thatcher which Diane had found out about. She was also angry that his involvement in the Equatorial Guinea coup pursued despite the danger it could have caused his family. Diane said: 'I think his choice not to pull out when he became suspicious showed his priorities. He was incredibly selfish, putting his own needs for self-fulfillment, greed and lust for power before his family.' Diane returned to America with the children. Thatcher planned to join them but his visa renewal application was rejected. Diane later went on to marry American statistician and sports card millionaire James Beckett in 2008.

After his enforced departure from South Africa Thatcher con-tinued to bleat about the injustice he suffered. He claimed his prosecution was politically inspired and that the country's President Thabo Mbeki had never liked his mother. Initially he went back home to mummy at her home in Chester Square in London's Belgravia. He then sought a place to live – his first choice of Monaco being thwarted when he was told – without further explanation – that just like his application for America, his temporary residency card would not be renewed.

He eventually settled in Spain with his second wife – Lady Francis Russell, formerly Sarah-Jane Russell, formerly Sarah-Jane Clemence – the woman with whom he had an affair while married to his first wife.

On 8 November 2009 it was reported that four days prior to his arrest in 2004 Thatcher met a South African intelligence figure for dinner in Pretoria to discuss his involvement in the coup. A source said Thatcher knew he was under investigation but did not believe he faced the risk of prosecution and therefore would not have needed to strike any deal. They confirmed Thatcher had supplied some information but denied reports he had offered to be a spy for South Africa to avoid prosecution over the case.

The repercussions of his actions will forever haunt Mark Thatcher. It was rumoured that kidnap squads were being gathered to snatch him away back to Equatorial Guinea to face a proper trial. (If the South African authorities require Thatcher to return to answer further questions – and he is legally obligated to do so – a kidnap operation would be much simpler.) The outcome of a guilty verdict could be up to thirty years in prison; by no means a prospect to savour. Equatorial Guinea's president Obiang could also decide to put a bounty on Thatcher's head and wait for someone to claim it. Despite his leniency for the public, in private he has always wanted Thatcher to go on trial declaring that Thatcher was 'a dirty player who lives his life getting himself involved in all sorts of dubious deals that are of benefit to himself . . . Mark Thatcher quickly jumped into this boat and became part and parcel of this plot.'

The country's attorney-general, Jose Olo Obono, has said that Thatcher will be hunted down 'wherever he goes'. Said one of Thatcher's friends: 'Personal security is a big concern. There are all sorts of people who would carry out that sort of things for money.'

It is no wonder that Thatcher's home, luxury villa Casa Flores, is hidden in dense forest on an almost inaccessible mountain plot above San Pedro de Alcantara, on Spain's Costa del Sol, and boasts incredible security measures. It is part of a complex called El Madronal, which has a central control room monitoring all movement twenty-four hours a day via a bank of CCTV screens. There are six electronic gates and no-one can gain access until their names, addresses and car registration numbers are logged. Another set of electronic gates protects every property, each of which has its own alarm system. But this is not a property owned by Thatcher but by Stephen Humberstone, a fellow Old-Harrovian who wants to evict his notorious tenant. Humberstone told *The Sunday Times*: 'Basically, he just pisses me off. He is always late with the rent. Under Spanish law I have to wait three months before I can take him to court and he presumably knows that and pays up after two months. We were in the same house at school – I can't believe he is treating me in such a shabby manner. He thinks a lot of himself. I think he likes the house because it is very secluded and a seven-minute drive from the main gate. Nobody would ever find him down there. He told me once he would like to buy it, but there is no way I would ever sell it to someone like him. If you see him, punch him on the nose from me, would you?'

Thatcher is still both a hunted and haunted man; his high-profile exploits having a devastating effect on any thoughts of a normal life. He applied for tax-residency status in Gibraltar, prompting speculation that he intended to make his home there but nothing seems to have come of his application.

As one observer summed up Thatcher's disasters: 'One looks in vain through Mark Thatcher's record for any solid achievement: everything he has has come through tail-coating his mother or somebody else's enterprise. If things went wrong, Mummy would get him off the hook. This time he tail-coated the wrong lot and Humpty-Dumpty fell right off the wall, so that not even Mummy has been able to put all the pieces together again.'

Chapter 7

'Tumbledown Tim'

A businessman was strongly implicated in the attempted coup. Indeed, he was named by Simon Mann as the main financier, providing $750,000, as having had secret discussions with exiled Equatorial Guinea president Severo Moto in his villa in Madrid (it was claimed the man also financed Moto in exile and was to be paid $16m to return him to power) and had a friendship with Sir Mark Thatcher. The businessman was described by Equatorial Guinea as central to the plan. It was also claimed that Mann had privately met him and another businessman weeks after the coup was aborted. There were reports of damning phone calls between Mark Thatcher and the man – and even between the man and disgraced MP Jeffrey Archer. The two men are said to have know each other since their days at Oxford. Archer was questioned over the phone calls between his home and 'Mr X' on the day several conspirators met in South Africa to finalise details of the coup. Archer's solicitors, while strenuously denying he had any knowledge of the plans, did, however confirm that two calls were made to his home from the businessman's phone. But, they said. Archer was away at the time and the calls were 'between different family members'.

Mann described the man as the 'overall boss' of the scheme, 'The Cardinal' and a man who had wrongly let him believe that the people of Equatorial Guinea desperately wanted the regime to tumble.

Equatorial Guinea's president Obiang, at one point said that 'The Cardinal' was secretly making plans to kill or kidnap Mann to silence him over the full details of the plot.

'The Cardinal's' alleged involvement also prompted the erroneous naming of other associates – such as Peter Mandelson to whom the man had lent his west London flat when Mandelson, then Northern Ireland Secretary, was forced to sell his own home after being involved in a scandal over undisclosed loans from fellow minister Geoffrey Robinson in 1996. Robinson resigned after reportedly lending Mandelson £373,000 to buy a property. The businessman hoped his friendship with Mandelson would help him become part of the British establishment. This was not to be when his connection with the Equatorial Guinea attempted coup became known and he became the focus of attention from the Equatorial Government – who wanted to sue him – and the South African police. It was no wonder that Mandelson issued a denial that the man had sounded him out over the coup plot. The allegation was also denied by 'The Cardinal'.

But just like every other aspect of the whole, sorry saga, there were conflicting 'facts'. In what was to become a notorious report drawn up by Nigel Morgan, a security consultant, Morgan said that Mandelson assured the businessman that he would 'get no problems from the British government side' over the plot and had invited the man to see him again 'if you need something done.' Morgan had interviewed the man and described him as 'very small and quite worn, looking tired and hunted. He had that swarthy Levantine look, but he's not a flamboyant character like Adnan Khashoggi. He's very sophisticated and quietly spoken.' Morgan noted that the businessman was void of any sense of humour.

The businessman had a strong incentive to climb on board the attempted coup – he would become chief oil broker in Equatorial Guinea. This was very tempting for the businessman, who had already made his fortune by trading in Nigerian oil – a fortune estimated at around £100m which had enabled him, amongst other assets, to acquire a £12m mansion in London's Chelsea.

The attention following the attempted coup did not please the businessman.

So just who is this mysterious – some might say murky-dealing-businessman embroiled in such a high-profile escapade? We would like to be able to name him – and indeed, it is not difficult to discovery his indentity – but there is much legal pressure on disconnecting him from Simon Mann and the attempted coup.

In the early days this 'Mr Big' counted the likes of a certain wealthy entrepreneurial set – Jimmy Goldsmith, John Aspinall and Mark Birley among his friends. He was later involved in a financial scandal with a bank which collapsed in 1984 amidst press allegations of misused funds.

The man is said to be worth around £100m. His lawyer once stated: 'We will vigorously defend the allegations, which are without foundation.'

But it is doubtful this businessman will suffer much from the aftermath of the attempted 2004 coup, once being described by a journalist as belonging to 'a small group of middlemen, a few dozen at most, who quietly grease the wheels of the global energy business, brokering transactions between oil companies and governments.'

A British judge ruled that Obiang could not bring any law suits against the man through lack of evidence, causing 'Mr X' to comment: 'It would have been fun. He accused me of causing him mental trauma and he would have been forced to come to court for a mental exam. He has tried every angle and opportunity and lost each time. You had an African dictator and some mercenaries and a shady Arab. It makes for a great novel, but the part of it that wasn't a novel was tested in court and proven to be wrong. The press has reported a pack of lies ... It's a joke, the whole story has been tested in six jurisdictions and the only place it is taken seriously is in Equatorial Guinea. The only so-called evidence is Simon Mann's testimony. I want to set the record straight and move on with my life.'

Tumbledown Tim

Former Scots Guard, Lieutenant-Colonel Tim Spicer is the 'individual' Jack Straw said was called into the Foreign Office in February 2004 to discuss the planned Equatorial Guinea coup. Spicer had said he had no knowledge of any plans to overthrow Obiang's regime.

Spicer was also the man who set up Sandline International with Simon Mann in 1995 and who also acted for the other private security company Executive Outcomes.

Writing about Spicer's exploits, journalist Duncan Campbell said: 'Although he agreed to be interviewed for this report, Spicer refused to discuss his operations for Sandline International. He had not complained, he said, about British newspaper reports that had accused him and Sandline of improper financial contracts including bribing government ministers. But "we thought about it" he said.'

Campbell also noted: 'Spicer was never fully signed up to the old-boys network that clusters in the confines of the Special Forces Club – an elite private social organization in central London whose membership is limited to serving and former members of the Special Forces and intelligence services from Britain, the United States and selected Allies. He would not say whether he had been refused membership. "I don't really discuss my personal life at all," he responded.'

Spicer's CV on his website is much more straightforward: 'During his 20 year military career he saw active service in Northern Ireland, the Falklands campaign, the Gulf war and Bosnia, as well as serving in the Far East, Cyprus and Germany. Tim's key appointments included Chief of Staff of an Armoured Brigade, Instructor at the Army Staff College, Staff Officer at the Directorate of Special Forces, Military Assistant to General Sir Peter de la Billiere, Military Assistant to General Sir Michael Rose in Bosnia and Commanding Officer of 1st Battalion Scots Guards. In 1992 Tim was awarded the OBE for operational service in Northern Ireland. During his military career he developed extensive knowledge of intelligence, counter terrorism, protective security and media relations. Since 1996 he has been at the forefront of the development of the private security industry worldwide and has been a very significant contributor to the debate over the industry's global contribution to government security initiatives.'

It was in 1992 that Spicer teamed up with Peter de la Billiere when he returned to London and took up the post of the British government's Middle East adviser. Spicer applied for the job as de la Billiere's military assistant and got the job. Soon after, Spicer contacted fellow ex-Scots Guards officer Simon Mann and 'co-opted' him into the operation. According to Spicer, de la Billiere and Mann were employed 'as liaison with the rulers of the Gulf States'. This was contested by a business associate of Mann's who said: 'British ambassadors were hired to do that job, and given the staff and resources to do so. Mann's real job was to help de la Billiere market the training services of twenty-two SAS and thus gain new clients for Britain's official mercenaries.' According to his autobiography,

Spicer moved down the corridor to work directly for the Director of Special Forces on 'highly-classified' projects. Like all others connected to the world of private security – or as some would say 'mercenaries for hire' – Spicer had always sought a less than orthodox military challenge. He was now doing just that.

Toward the end of Spicer's stint in the Special Forces Mann offered him a military contract in Angola, which Spicer declined. Instead, he continued his military career until early 1995, finally being employed as spokesman for former SAS commander General Michael Rose, then head of the UN protection force in Bosnia.

In 1995, Executive Outcomes was called on to help seize back control from rebels of Angola's oil installations in Soyo. Troops were ferried to Angola from a small airport near Johannesburg.

With a ban declared in South Africa on private security forces and their operations constantly coming under scrutiny, Spicer joined a lunchtime meeting in October 1996 with Simon Mann and Tony Buckingham to discuss a 'fresh start.' Executive Outcomes was relaunched as Sandline International.

In 1997 Spicer's intervention in Papua New Guinea saw him arriving with 70 hired guns, mainly South Africans, to attack rebels on the detached island of Bougainville, home to the world's largest and most lucrative copper mine, recover it and restore it to operation. But the $36m contract – the operation was codenamed Operation Oyster – was leaked to the PNG army which rebelled against Sandline's 'invaders'. Spicer was arrested with $400,000 in cash on him. His Sandline company was accused of having made corrupt payments through a Swiss bank account to Mathias Ijape, then the defence minister of Papua New Guinea. Spicer was detained for nearly a month and underwent a trial to 'show the corruption' involved in the contract. During the proceedings. He was later released with help from the British government and sued the Papua New Guinea government for money he said he had not been paid. Following the scandal, the country's prime minister, Julius Chan, resigned, and his government collapsed.

In 1998 Spicer's company Sandline was contracted by ousted president of Sierra Leone, Ahamed Kabbah, to restore his country's government. This involved training around 40,000 soldiers and a deal with an Indian banker called Rakesh Saxena to supply 30 tons of Bulgarian arms. But supplying arms to Sierra Leone violated United

81

Nations sanctions. Spicer always denied that he or his company did anything illegal. He said he and his company were 'if anything victims of a wider UK political controversy. The British government knew of the action, which did not contravene international law or the UN Security Council's arms embargo. The facts are borne out by a Government investigation, two inquiries and a UN Legal opinion.' The reward for Spicer's efforts was said to be $10m in diamond mine concessions. In February 1999 a parliamentary report found that Foreign Office officials and diplomats had withheld information from the government about Sandline's plans to export arms to Sierra Leone in violation of United Nations sanctions.

Spicer was called in by the Sri Lankan government in 2001 to quell the infamous Tamil Tigers bloody terrorist war.

Spicer said of his work: 'Mercenary is an interesting word. But I object to the image it conjures up. In most cases it is derogatory. It implies ill-discipline and thuggery. We shy away from that image. Discipline and performance-wise, the people we employ have to be of a level of a First World army.'

Timothy Simon Spicer was born in Aldershot – the same military town as Simon Mann – in 1952. Like Mann too, he attended public school and was to follow his father into the British Army.

By his own confession Spicer spent his late teens 'drifting around the world.' This included a stint of bumming around America. When he returned to Britain he decided against going to university, but took a law course – which he failed. Spicer also failed on his first attempt to pass the British Army officers' selection board but passed on his second attempt. He was dispatched to train at the elitist Sandhurst Royal Military Academy, where after six months, he won the Academy's Sword of Honour for best cadet. Spicer was then commissioned into the highly-respected Scots Guards.

Spicer served as a captain in the Falkland Islands when Argentina invaded in 1982 and nearly died when an artillery shell exploded on Mount Tumbledown, one of the last Argentinian strongholds before the capture of Port Stanley. Spicer earned the nickname 'Tumbledown Tim'. One of his colleagues said of him: 'He was the most arrogant, pompous bastard I have ever met.'

Spicer also served in Northern Ireland from 1992 to 1993 – service which earned him an OBE. It also earned him notoriety for Spicer was the commanding officer of two Scots Guards, Mark Wright and

James Fisher, who shot and killed 18-year-old civilian Peter McBride in north Belfast on 4 September 1992. McBride was unarmed and had been running away. Spicer stood by his soldiers even after they were convicted of murder and sentenced to life imprisonment on 10 February 1995. He said the soldiers had legitimately believed their lives to be in peril. (Wright and Fisher were released from Maghaberry Prison on 2 September 1998 as part of the Good Friday Agreement.) In his autobiography, Spicer said the two soldiers should have been sent back on patrol immediately after the fatal shooting, 'under the same principle as getting straight back on a horse when you have been thrown off.'

Officially, Spicer left Sandline in 1999 but the company was in operation until 2004. A note left on the closed office doors read: 'The general lack of governmental support for Private Military Companies willing to help end armed conflicts in places like Africa, in the absence of effective international intervention, is the reason for this decision. Without such support the ability of Sandline to make a positive difference in countries where there is widespread brutality and genocidal behaviour is materially diminished.'

In 2000, Spicer launched Crisis and Risk Management. In 2001, he changed the company's name to Strategic Consulting International and set up a partner firm specializing in anti-piracy consulting, called Trident Maritime. In 2002, Spicer established Aegis Defence Services, which around the beginning of the Iraq war was consulting for the Disney Cruise Line. Spicer's website extols all that he has done with the company: 'Since the formation of Aegis in 2002, Tim has over-seen the rapid growth of the company. In addition to leading Aegis's growth, Tim spearheaded the company's bid in 2004 for the $300m prime US Government tender to provide core reconstruction security support services in Iraq. This contract was the largest ever US Department of Defence contract awarded in this sector. He has also developed a number of innovative aspects of support which have been adopted by the Coalition.

'Tim's strengths in the conceptual development of operations and planning, and his deep insight into the needs of the sector's client base, have helped deliver increasing market share, constant customer satisfaction and the growing enhancement of Aegis's reputation.

'He created the Aegis Charitable Foundation in 2004, a registered UK charity which provides direct assistance to communities through low cost, high impact civil affairs projects. Tim's effort and support of this charity not only significantly helps communities in great need having suffered from conflict, but has also enhanced the ability of Reconstruction Operations in Iraq to actually implement their programmes successfully. Tim's concept for the charity has been to carefully target projects that communities need and also want. The Foundation has therefore concentrated its efforts on building relationships with local tribal leaders and communities to provide clean water projects, inoculation programmes, school and health clinic equipment and smaller items such as toys, clothes and shoes. Tim has now expanded the Foundation's arena to include Afghanistan.'

That same year, 2004, Spicer found he was back involved with his old partner Mann – albeit inadvertently when he was summoned to tell what he knew about the proposed Equatorial Guinea Coup.

Chapter 8

Black Days in Black Beach

Mann was released from Chikurubi prison on 9 May 2007 only to be re-arrested to comply with the extradition order. The whole business got murkier. The day after Omega Mugambate made the extradition order and the same day as she refused an application for Mann to be allowed bail, Zimbabwe's biggest hotel and leisure group signed a multimillion dollar deal to develop seaside tourism in Equatorial Guinea. Zimbabwe's president Robert Mugabe later announced a 'friendship delegation' would be visiting the country. And on 14 May, with Mann back in jail, his lawyer Jonathan Samkange was arrested on a charge of violating immigration laws. He was freed the next day and the charges were dropped. (A few months later, lawyer Fabian Nsue Nguema who had defended a group of the South African mercenaries was suspended for a year by the Bar Association of Equatorial Guinea. He received no notice of any allegations against him or given a chance to defend himself. But he was told that the decision to suspend him from working for a year was made in collaboration with the government because his conduct at the infamous trial 'fell short of international fair trial standards'.)

In June 2007, *The Mail on Sunday* newspaper was allowed access to Black Beach prison where Nick du Toit and other co-conspirators were incarcerated. The newspaper said this access was allowed because the authorities were keen to show conditions of the newly-built prison (with its hospital wing and pharmacy) compared to those of the old one. Just eight months old, the building was described as having yellow-painted functional buildings separated by a concrete exercise yard, cordoned off from 'a huge expanse of sea by barbed-wire fencing . . . prisoners were lounging there, several of them playing *jeu de dames*, a board game similar to draughts. Others squatted in the intense heat, chickens pecking around them. In the single-storey infirmary are ten beds on a newly-tiled floor. Close by is the canteen where twenty prisoners at a time take their meals. Stacks of blue and purple plastic mugs and dishes were piled high on the kitchen surfaces, the walls freshly whitewashed. The air conditioning was a surprise. Outside the midday temperature had hit 30°C (86°F). In the main building, the ground floor is one huge hallway with communal cells feeding of it. Some prisoners use money given to them by their families to send out for sweets, chocolates, crisps, soap and other "luxuries" which they sell for a small profit at a makeshift stall. Up a steep wrought-iron staircase is the first-floor landing with mire mesh to guard against suicides. Some prisoners had painted a jokey *"No moleste"* – Spanish for "Do not disturb" – on their cell doors. They were quiet, subdued, watching us with their dead eyes. Eighty prisoners are incarcerated at Black Beach.'

The newspaper also secured an interview with Obiang's lawyer Harry Page who said extradition was 'a desirable situation for a number of reasons: firstly to identify the financiers of the conspiracy; secondly to expose others, including foreign government officials who may have been a party to it; and thirdly to discourage such acts in the future . . . Simon Mann's right of defence will be respected and I believe he will be properly treated. His extradition may prove to be the key to enable this whole sorry episode to be brought to an end.'

This prompted Mann's lawyer Jonathan Samkange to say: 'There are many wheels within wheels in this case. Even the documents read like an adventure novel. Once Simon was arrested I travelled to London for meetings with politicians to see if they could help him. It would not be helpful to him at present to name names, but this is one of his current dilemmas. While he is feeling bitter, and determined to spread the blame, he is nervous about revealing everything to the Equatorial Guinea authorities. He has never admitted his part in the coup and to do so now would be incriminating. This is a difficult time for Simon.'

In January 2008 Mann lodged an appeal against his extradition to Equatorial Guinea. Jonathan Samkange said: 'We have a strong case. Mr Mann is extremely sick. We fear he will not get a fair trial in Equatorial Guinea, and to remove him is unlawful. Even Mugabe (Zimbabwe's president) does not want to be breaking the law in the full glare of international publicity. But we are at the mercy of what the politicians want. Our chances are dependent not on the law but on the Zimbabwean government and where there is political interference there is no justice. He should have been deported to the UK when his sentence expired under the law.' Mann was deported to Equatorial Guinea in secret, leading to claims by his lawyers that the extradition was hastened to prevent him appealing to the Zimbabwe Supreme Court. Mann's deportation was furtive and dramatic. It was reported that he was snatched by Mugabe's soldiers from his cell during the night and his cries for help went unheeded. According to some inmates and prison officers, Mann struggled with the soldiers and was punched before being dragged outside and bundled into a white Nissan 4×4 vehicle with blacked out windows. His glasses were lost in the struggle and he was wedged in the vehicle still shackled. Escorted by three other vehicles containing armed soldiers, Mann was taken to the Manyame air force base just south of Harare, where a jet was waiting to fly him through the night to Equatorial Guinea. Apparently, then followed an almost farcical situation as the Zimbabwean forces started arguing over what to do with Mann and a fight broke out between officers charged with handing him over. In a country where money talks, some wanted to fly Mann to another destination where they could keep him hostage for a huge ransom. Gun shots were even reported to have been heard. It was more than four hours before Mann finally got onto the plane (which was operating illegally and had not registered a flight plan) with his departure timed just after 5am.

Said Mann's wife Amanda: 'I can't stand to think of him being as frightened as he must have been when they finally did take him or how frightened he must be now. Simon does not deserve this. We have to get him out of there. I need my husband back, and my children desperately need their father.'

Meanwhile, concern for Mann's plight was being raised in Parliament back in London. On 7 February 2008 – the day after Mann was visited in prison by US ambassador David Johnson and his deputy

Anton Smith after Equatorial Guinea refused entry to the British consul – eight MPs, headed by Lord Bingham of Cornhill, managed to stop the hearing into Mann's case because of Equatorial Guinea's refusal to guarantee his welfare and legal rights. Jose Olo Obono, the attorney general of Equatorial Guinea, had sought the right to claim compensation from Mann and his alleged co-plotters. The request had been rejected by the High Court and Appeal Court on the grounds that it was beyond the jurisdiction of British law. Lord Bingham told Obono that the hearing would be adjourned until assurances could be given about Mann's rights to see a lawyer. The attorney general was also told that Equatorial Guinea would have to pay for all the time wasted as a result of the adjournment. The British consul in Lagos travelled to Malabo and visited Mann in prison on 12 February.

There was concern over what was seen as the 'kidnap' of Mann from Zimbabwe to Equatorial Guinea. Conservative MPs voiced those concerns. Julian Lewis, Tory MP for New Forest East (the constituency in which Mann's Hampshire home 'Inchmery' was located), made the following statement: 'My constituent Mr Simon Mann has completed his jail sentence in Zimbabwe but has been transferred by the Mugabe regime to a potentially terrible fate in Equatorial Guinea, despite the fact that his appeals processes have not been completed and despite the assurances given by the British ambassador to Zimbabwe that that would not happen. May we have a statement as soon as possible on the Floor of the House from the Foreign Secretary about what action is going to be taken? Quiet diplomacy has failed and we now have to save Mr Mann, whatever he has or has not done, from torture and a horrible death in a terrible situation.' Dr Lewis tabled the Commons thus:

To ask the Secretary of State for Foreign and Commonwealth Affairs

(1) What steps he plans to take in the week beginning 31 March to monitor the (a) treatment and (b) risk of torture of Mr Simon Mann in Black Beach Prison, Equatorial Guinea; and whether Mr Mann is still being continuously shackled.
(2) What steps he plans to take in the week beginning 7 April to monitor the (a) treatment and (b) risk of torture of Mr Simon Mann in Black Beach Prison, Equatorial Guinea.

(3) What steps he plans to take in the week beginning 14 April to monitor the *(a)* treatment and *(b)* risk of torture of Mr Simon Mann in Black Beach Prison, Equatorial Guinea.

He was answered by Meg Munn, British Labour Co-operative politician who said: 'Our consul from the British deputy high commission in Lagos was refused consular access to Simon Mann during his last visit to Equatorial Guinea in March. We have expressed our concern to the Equatorial Guinea authorities and are urgently seeking another consular visit. The authorities have offered assurances that Mr Mann will be treated well whilst in detention. His welfare remains our primary concern.'

Richard Benyon (Newbury) demanded that the ambassador or other representative of Equatorial Guinea be called in and told that Mann had a right to a free and fair trial. Henry Bellingham (North-West Norfolk) pointed out that Mann had two sons serving in the British Army and said Mann had been kidnapped 'wholly unlawfully' from Zimbabwe. James Clappison (Hertsmere) and John Whittingdale (Maldon and Chelmsford East) also made representations on Mann's behalf, which Harriet Harman, as Leader of the House, said she would pass on to the Foreign Office.

Mann was also supported by MP Vince Cable who put forward an Early Day Motion about Mann's treatment in prison which received backing from several parties. Lord Maginnis of Drumglass asked:

Further to the Written Answer by Lord Malloch-Brown on 21 February (WA 80-1), whether they were informed by the Zimbabwean authorities of the imminent extradition of Simon Mann from Zimbabwe to Equatorial Guinea immediately prior to his being extradited; what response they had from the Zimbabwean authorities regarding their obligations under the International Covenant on Civil and Political Rights; and what contact they have had with Simon Mann since his extradition.

Lord Malloch-Brown (Minister of State, Foreign and Commonwealth Office) replied: 'Further to the answer I gave the noble Lord on 21 February, we were not informed by the Zimbabwean authorities of the imminent removal of Simon Mann from Zimbabwe to Equatorial Guinea immediately prior to his removal. The Zimbabwean authorities have since told us that they believe they complied with their international obligations in this case. Our Deputy High Commission in Lagos provides consular assistance to British nationals in Equatorial Guinea.'

Mann was certainly not without his supporters. Friends of Prince William started a 'Free Simon Mann' campaign on the social networking website Facebook. In just a few days, more than 1,500 people had added their names.

On 8 March 2008, Britain's Channel 4 television station won a legal battle to broadcast an interview with Mann during which he named British political figures including ministers and others involved in the coup attempt. Mann's wife Amanda had originally won a High Court Injunction to stop the interview being shown. Through her lawyer, Anthony Kerman, Amanda said the her husband's allegations had been made 'under duress.' Kerman's statement read: 'We believe that Mr Mann's interests could be irreparably harmed if the broadcast takes place. I haven't seen the piece but we do believe that there may be admissions which he makes against his own interests and there may be allegations in the piece too. Channel 4 says that he talks frankly about the events leading up to his arrest. I'm told by other people that he may have said considerably more than that, but that is sufficient for me to be very concerned.' The injunction was called for because 'it is not apparent he [Mann] could properly consent to the interview taking place.' Kerman was acting on the 'general instructions' of Amanda Mann but not of Mann himself. He was reported to be a close associate of the businessman Mann had named as being involved in the coup. The programme was broadcast on 11 March.

Mann said tacit approval for a regime change in Equatorial Guinea had come from Washington, the CIA and big US oil companies. In fact, Mann probably misunderstood their silence as approval. He further implicated senior members of the Equatorial Guinea army, police and government, saying he had been supplied with details of Obiang's daily movements and his health problems. Commented *The Independent on Sunday* about the attempted coup: 'Inconspicuous is not a word that leaps to mind, which in turn, suggests possible explanations. It was either a bafflingly naïve diversion for a team so steeped in the ways of Africa to make. Or the conspirators thought the necessary people in Zimbabwe had been squared.'

Francisco Macias Nguema, who rose from being a humble clerk to the first president of Equatorial Guinea – and a brutal leader. In 1979 he was overthrown by Teodoro Obiang Nguema Mbasogo and later executed in September of the same year.

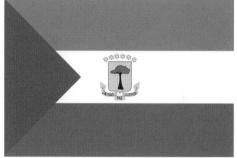

The national flag of Equatorial Guinea.

A stamp showing Francisco Macias Nguema.

2 PTAS GUINEANAS

12·OCTUBRE·1969

CORREOS •

1ER ANIVº INDEPENDENCIA

REPUBLICA DE GUINEA ECUATORIAL

Nick du Toit who paid the price for recruiting mercenaries in the attempted coup, and was imprisoned.

A gaunt Simon Mann pictured during his prison term.

Inside Black Beach prison – Equatorial Guinea's government insist conditions have improved following criticism.

An aerial view of Chikurubi Prison in Harare, South Africa.

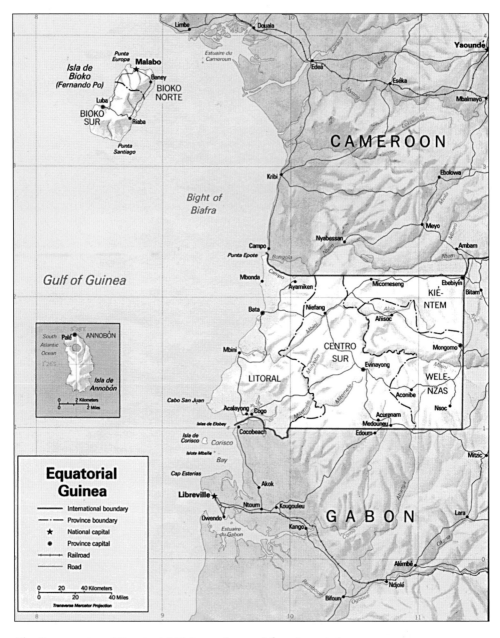

The tiny country of Equatorial Guinea – focus of the attempted coup.

Mercenaries employed by the company Executive Outcomes.

Despite claims that there is vast renovation going on in Equatorial Guinea's capital of Malabo, many people are without water and electricity.

On trial. Simon Mann and fellow prisoners during the opening proceedings in Equatorial Guinea.

A group of the attempted coup mercenaries shortly after their arrest.

Equatorial Guinea's President Nguema with US Secretary Condoleezza Rice.

The reality of time in prison. A cramped cell.

Exiled Severo Moto who hoped to take over leadership of Equatorial Guinea.

Mark Thatcher who claims to have unwittingly financed the attempted coup.

Simon Mann – the whole escapade took its toll.

Mann spoke openly about events leading up to his arrest. He said he had been the 'manager, not the architect' of the plot. He talked about the involvement of others such as the businessman, saying it was he who was the main force behind the mission. Said Mann: 'I was involved and I was if you like, the manager. Below me were a lot of people including those arrested with me in Zimbabwe? Above me in the machine were other people.' The named man still denied any involvement and issued another statement: 'I have a great deal of sympathy for Simon Mann's predicament. I'm sure he is in considerable distress. He has made many contradictory statements. The only statement he has made freely was an affidavit in Zimbabwe in which he confirmed that his original allegations about me were made under duress. That is the only statement of his which is reliable. I can confirm that I had no involvement in or responsibility for the alleged coup.' There were rumours that disgraced Tory peer Lord Archer was also involved, but Mann – and Archer – denied it. The claim had arisen after a deposit of $135,000 was made into Mann's Channel Island company Logistics, four days before the failed coup. The payment was made in the name of 'J.H. Archer'. Mann insisted it was not THAT J. Archer and a statement issued by Archer's lawyers said he had no 'prior knowledge' of the alleged coup. Some felt this did not answer the claim about money being paid into Mann's account, but all Archer's lawyer John Dickinson would add was: 'Lord Archer does not want to expand on that statement. He believes it covers all issues.'

Even Labour minister Peter Mandelson was wrongly mentioned in connection with the plot – probably because they were both friends of the 'Mr Big' businessman. It was alleged that Mann had privately met the man and another businessman accused of involvement in the coup, weeks after it was aborted. ('Mr Big' had also offered his West London flat to Mr Mandelson when the former Northern Ireland Secretary was embroiled in a scandal of an undisclosed loan from fellow Minister Geoffrey Robinson.) Mann stated categorically that neither Archer nor Mandelson were involved, saying: 'They've no involvement at all. God knows where that came from.'

Mann insisted that he would co-operate with the authorities of Equatorial Guinea, saying: 'I have been helping the authorities as best I can with this sorry story ... Here I am accused of terrible things when nothing happened. The intent was there, but it was a fuck up. I am actually a victim of a far more serious crime than any crime I have committed … I am sorry, I have been saying for four years that I am sorry. I should write that on my forehead.' Perhaps as a crucial sop to his captors (the Attorney General and Security Minister were sitting in on the interview) Mann told the programme that he had been misled about problems in Equatorial Guinea. He said he had been told conditions were 'diabolically bad' and that despite warnings to the contrary, he had NOT been tortured, adding: 'I have been treated well. My accommodation is good; there's water, there's food and I am under no coercion.'

In a strange analogy of his plight, Mann said: 'If we go mountain-eering, leaving the people down in base camp who have sponsored the expedition and who are with us. If we get caught up on the mountain in an avalanche and if those people down there, who I think are my friends, roll their sleeping bags up, put their tents down and go off back to London, then I can tell you one thing, they had better hope and pray that I don't get back off that mountain because if I do they're going to get an ice axe right between the eyes.'

In that same interview, Obiang called Mann 'a criminal bastard'. A spokesman for the television company said: 'We would not be intending to broadcast this interview if it were not in accordance with Mr Mann's wishes. This is responsible reporting.'

The Mail on Sunday newspaper obtained exclusive pictures of Mann being interviewed by *Channel 4 News* foreign affairs corres-pondent Jonathan Miller. It reported: 'He appears to be in good health and the jail is obviously clean and hygienic … And would it not be better to keep him at the forefront of the public conscience by allowing the broadcast, which shows him looking well? … Mann appears fit, healthy and in good humour, laughing and joking … The prison is clean and freshly painted, and although Mann is shackled and handcuffed, his jailers have taken care to wind cloth around his leg irons so the metal does not rub against his skin. They have also removed his shoelaces, for fear he could use them to hang himself.' Descried as journalism of significant public interest, the interview with Mann lasted around forty-five minutes and a spokesman said: 'At first he was reluctant, but as it progressed, he opened up. He was asked repeatedly if he had been coerced and he said "no", and whether he was speaking of his own free will and he said "yes".'

Writing on the World Socialist Web Site, Ann Talbot reported: 'Mann appeared wearing handcuffs and leg irons padded with rags. The camera lingered on the visible welts on Mann's wrists as he claimed that he was being well treated in prison. With his thumbs moving nervously, he said that he had been put under no coercion. Channel 4 reporter Jonathan Miller made it clear that the attorney general of Equatorial Guinea and heavily-armed guards were in the room throughout the interview.'

It was later claimed by Equatorial Guinea's Minister of Security, Manuel Nguema Mbo, that Mann had been put in a private room with an exercise machine and a collection of books sent by his family and was also allowed weekly phone calls home. Mbo said: 'I think it is fair to say that he is not having such a bad time. We have lunch together most days and enjoy a glass of wine.'

This preferential treatment, apparently in 'reward' for Mann's co-operation brought new anxieties. His lawyers feared things would change once he was found guilty. 'He is a celebrity prisoner and has had a lot in his hand to bargain with,' said Fabien Nsula who represented six local men also on remand over the alleged plot and who claimed they had been beaten. 'Simon Mann was able to negotiate treatment that is by no means normal in that place. But now that he has given them [the authorities] what they want, there is no guarantee it will continue.' One observer commented: 'I think there will be a lot of animosity against the white man who planned this all and yet gets treated like a lord. I would warn him to watch his back.'

That month Crause Steyl quietly returned to his home in South Africa, expecting to be arrested. Instead, the Directorate of Special Operations, an elite crime squad known as the 'Scorpions', offered him a deal: immunity in return for complete co-operation. Steyl was angered by the way his friends Mann and du Toit had been left to their fate with so little support and decided to tell all. He was convinced that Thatcher too was in on the plot from the beginning.

Later in March 2008, Ponciano Mbomio Nvo, the Spanish-trained lawyer called in to defend Mann, gave an interview to the *Daily Telegraph*. He made his feeling clear over the impossibility of a fair trial: 'All the judges in this country are from the family or the party of the president. There is no judge or judgement which is neutral.

They are only there to defend the interests of the president and his family ... as a lawyer I don't accept he's guilty, I can't accept that. He has declared he is guilty but at the judicial level there's nothing. For us lawyers, what is not in the proceedings does not exist in the legal world – TV, newspapers, internet, they don't exist.'

Mr Nvo had a personal interest in Mann's fate. He himself had spent three years in Black Beach under Franciso Macias, the predecessor of Obiang. (Macias was deposed by Obiang on 3 August 1979 in a bloody coup, placed on trial and sentenced to death. He was executed on 29 September 1979 by a firing squad.) Mr Nvo added: 'The government has promised not to kill or touch him and since he arrived here he's been well treated. I have been informed that the extradition is not in accordance with the law. There was no extradition treaty between Zimbabwe and Equatorial Guinea when he was arrested and it cannot be made retrospective ... he will be found guilty because they want to justify the extradition ... the intention of the president is that Mr Mann implicates lots of people, especially Severo Moto. The president wants to show the international community that there was a criminal act against him. After one year, two years, three years he can decree a pardon and send him to his country. The government's greater aim is the imprisonment of Severo Moto. What's he going to do with Mr Mann? He's English; he can't be president of Equatorial Guinea. But Severo Moto wants to be president. He is his enemy.'

Moto was sentenced in Equatorial Guinea in his absence to sixty-two years for his alleged part in the failed coup.

His plans to regain his place as leader of troubled Equatorial Guinea had failed. The plan to fly him in from Spain and then get him back into power once Obiang's regime had been toppled. Spanish oil companies lost out to US companies in the bid for oil concessions there and some political observers feel a regime change might have been the best way of regaining Spanish influence in the former colony. Spain, therefore, had something to gain from ousting Obiang. It is rumoured that a Spanish warship was sighted off the coast of Equatorial Guinea as the plot was about to begin.

It did not, of course, work out as was planned. And in a BBC interview, Justice Minister Ruben Mangue pointed the finger at Moto as the man behind the attempted coup. Moto said the president was just trying to damage his reputation: 'I have absolutely nothing to do with this story. I believe that once again in the face of my announcement of my return to Equatorial Guinea, President Obiang has become nervous and of course he has no trouble plotting and preparing traps like this in order to tarnish my political career and really keep the population on tenterhooks.'

Severo Moto was born on 6 November 1943 in Spanish Guinea. Being of the same Mongomo clan as Equatorial Guinea's leaders Francisco Macías Nguema and Obiang, Moto was allowed to participate in government activities during the 1970s and 1980s. He was a radio operator in the early 1970s, later rising to the post of minister for tourism and information under both Macias and his successor (1971–76, 79–82). The fact that he served for eleven years under both rulers as a government minister is often forgotten by those who see him as an opposition leader. He claims to have won several elections in Equatorial Guinea. He is reportedly on good terms with José María Aznar, the former premier of Spain.

Moto lost his government position in Equatorial Guinea with the end of the military dictatorship in 1982.

With the advent of multi-party democracy in the early eighties, Moto founded the Progress Party of Equatorial Guinea. Moto's opposition to Obiang saw him imprisoned at Malabo's notorious Black Beach prison.

Moto fled to Spain in 1986 where he established a government in exile, to the annoyance of Teodoro Obiang.

Following the attempted coup involving Simon Mann in 2004, Moto was arrested and flown straight back to Spain. In his absence he was sentenced to sixty-two years in prison.

Moto disappeared for a short time in 2005 and then suddenly re-appeared. He claimed a pair of hit men had taken him out on a yacht in Dubrovnik, Croatia, only to let him go because he was a fellow Roman Catholic.

Moto enjoyed refugee status since the Spanish government granted it in 1986. But the government revoked the status in 2005 in the belief that Moto was using Spain as the base for attempted coups on Equatorial Guinea. This led to Moto launching a series of appeals that ultimately took him to the Supreme Court. Moto stated that before being expelled to a third country he would return to Equatorial Guinea in order to call for free elections. He appealed against the decision, and eventually, in March 2008, the Spanish Supreme Court upheld his asylum request.

In April 2008, Moto was arrested after weapons were found in a car at the Spanish port of Sagunto on 4 March that year. The weapons were reportedly about to be sent to Equatorial Guinea. At the National Court, Judge Fernando Andreu outlined an eight-page document linking Moto with the arms haul. He said: 'From wire-tapped telephone conversations, it's deduced that Severo Moto was not only fully aware of the purchase and shipment of the weapons to Equatorial Guinea, but that he coordinated and gave instructions to the others to carry out that trafficking.' Spanish police had found an assault rifle, a rifle, a pistol, a semiautomatic pistol magazine and numerous boxes of ammunition for various weapons. Police alleged the operation included a man from Equatorial Guinea, acting on Moto's behalf to obtain a vehicle, and two Spanish men – one to move the vehicle to Sagunto port and another to fund the operation. In return, Moto allegedly promised the financier favorable business treatment in Equatorial Guinea if Moto eventually came to power there.

Moto was sentenced to four months in prison in Spain for allegedly trafficking arms to Equatorial Guinea

After his release, Moto said he was innocent of the charges and said he had felt let down that Spain had colluded with his enemy Obiang whom he described as a 'murderous dictator' and whom had put pressure on to ensure a prosecution.

Moto said: 'I want to express my disappointment and surprise at the behaviour of the Spanish authorities over my detention. It was a politically motivated move by the Spanish secret service. Not only was I arrested without a warrant, I was sent to jail without trial and until further notice. I'm a political prisoner.' Moto added that he had only been released after supporters posted 10,000 Euros bail.

He said that his 'government-in-exile' feared that an attempt would be made on their lives and had requested round the clock protection from Spanish authorities. 'I am haunted even in Spain by the long murderous arm of Obiang', Moto said confirming that a letter had been sent to Spain's Prime Minister Jose Luis Zapatero but that 'we have not yet received a reply from the Spanish government. But we would welcome one.'

Spain's present Socialist Party government has been less favourable towards Moto than the right-wing Popular Party government, in power at the time the abortive coup was in preparation. But the Spanish High Court still refused a bid by Equatorial Guinea to have Moto extradited and has confirmed his asylum status.

Chapter 9

Courting the Enemy

Mann's trial started on 18 June 2008. The day before, *The Sunday Times* told how Equatorial Guinea was on 'high alert' for the proceedings. 'There are soldiers on the streets of Equatorial Guinea's steamy little capital, patrol vessels cruising offshore and extra checks at entry points ... President Teodorao Obiang Nguema who has ruled with an iron first for thirty years insists that such measures are warranted.' Obiang said security was paramount for Mann, a prisoner of 'high quality and importance.' Getting a trial at all was something Mann should have been grateful for. It was only his high-profile that ensured this. For many others before him, not being under a global spotlight had meant they were at the mercy of Obiang's so-called legal process. As Amnesty International findings confirmed: 'The law provides for an independent judiciary, however, the government did not respect this provision in practice. Judges served at the pleasure of the president, and they were appointed, transferred and dismissed for political reasons. Judicial corruption was widespread.' In December 2004, Obiang fired a judge and two clerks for incompetence.

Equatorial Guinea's court system is composed of lower provincial courts, two appeals courts, a military tribunal and the Supreme Court. There are around sixty judges in the country of whom around twenty per cent are trained lawyers. Some defendants are tried without being present. For Mann's trial, almost the entire diplomatic community of Equatorial Guinea was invited – around thirty people – plus seventy-five other dignitaries who had been especially invited with one admitting they did not really know why, adding: 'We are entering uncharted waters here. Rubber sandals were handed out to people whose shoes were deemed "suspicious". There was a strong police presence.'

The first day was spent on opening proceedings, both the prosecution and defence case, conducted in a language Mann did not understand. At the start of the trial one of the three magistrates noticed that Mann's ankles were shackled and ordered that they be removed. It took twenty minutes for a key to be found. The scenes were recorded by *Channel 4 News* with correspondent Sue Turton being allowed access in court to Mann. She asked if he was ready for the trial and he replied he was like a 'coiled spring, ready to leap into action.' He admitted he was hoping for clemency. Mann sat in the middle of a group of co-conspirators, all dressed in a grey prison uniform with blue and white striped pockets. Channel 4 was lucky to get their exclusive insight. No other journalists were allowed to take cameras – or even notebooks – into court. Yet when the press entered the room they were initially allowed to stroll over to where Mann sat with other defendants on a rank of fixed seats on one side of the court. Before they were moved away, Mann was asked if he had been treated well. He smiled and said, 'yes, from the beginning'. Mann was even allowed to walk slowly to the public toilet in the foyer accompanied by only one guard. But before the three black-cloaked judges took their place at the long table, beneath a huge chandelier, the men were then moved to the front two rows of the auditorium and on plush red chairs.

In court, Mann reiterated his version of events; that Mark Thatcher 'was not just an investor' but came 'on board completely', knew the businessman and had been in contact with Severo Moto, that the businessman was the 'overall boss' and known as 'The Cardinal', that the attempted coup 'became like a military operation because the Spanish and South African governments were both giving the green light' and that 'their involvement was clandestine and they will never admit it', that 'The Cardinal' had misled him into believing that the people of Equatorial Guinea were deeply dissatisfied with Obiang and that the country was ripe for a revolution.

Mann said that the coup was hastily organised as it had to be carried out before the Spanish elections on 14 March 2004 because the plotters believed that the centre-right government of Prime Minister Jose Maria Aznar (who served from 1994 to 2004) would fall and the incoming administration might not fulfil the promises of diplomatic and military support which had been made. Said Mann: 'Everything was in a big hurry because we had this date of 14 March, the Spanish election, which was coming closer and closer. I had been told by X that the Aznar government had promised immediate diplomatic recognition if Severo Moto took over.' He added that the Spanish government had promised to send a contingent of Guardia Civil and provide logistical support. Mann also claimed that an intelligence contact had asked him to provide Moto's telephone number so that South African president, Thabo Mbeki, could speak to the man hailed as the next president of Equatorial Guinea. A spokesman for Spain's Foreign Ministry denied the claims saying: 'We did not give the green light to any of this.' Any involvement was also denied by South African officials.

In court Mann confessed: 'I am very, very sorry for what I have done. I am also happy that we failed. I think that the people that were seriously involved in this and have not faced justice, well they should do so now.'

There was allegedly a key document produced at Mann's trial – the 'Contract for a Coup' which was said to comprise two agreements between 'Captain F' (Simon Mann and referring to his middle name of Francis) and Severo Moto, one of which said Mann would be paid $15m plus all expenses involved in the coup. The papers were said to be signed by Mann.

The trial lasted five days. It ended without a verdict and with the president of the court not indicating when there would be one. In its closing moments Mann had stood up and launched an attack on members of his legal team. He claimed that in 2005 he was offered a deal by Equatorial Guinea's Attorney General which would see him avoid trial in exchange for naming 'Mr Big' and Thatcher in an affidavit, but that his lawyers had advised him not to accept the offer. He said a similar offer was made in 2006 but that he was again advised not to take it. Asked in court why his lawyers gave the advice Mann replied: 'You would have to ask them.'

Mann's lawyer, Jose Pablo Nvo, had made an impassioned plea for clemency saying Mann had 'collaborated fully' with authorities and that he was a 'victim' and a 'pawn in a game played by powerful people' to bring down Obiang and install Moto. Added Nvo: 'His ceaseless attitude of repentance, his total collaboration and his

100

sincere desire to repair the damage he had sought to inflict on Equatorial Guinea deserved to be considered during sentencing. He is in jail, in Africa, cut off from his family and friends and he doesn't speak the language.'

As the judges retired to consider their verdict (which took nearly two weeks) Jose Olo Obono named Thatcher and Mr X the business-man as his next targets for prosecution saying: 'I am not going to sit here with my arms folded, but there were obstacles in the Simon Mann Case and it has taken four years to bring him to justice. It may be a long haul but we will bring the others to justice.' He added that the prosecution would 'Demonstrate through Simon Mann's own statements the level of participation of each of the people implicated in this affair, which was orchestrated from beginning to end by Simon Mann.'

The businessman linked to the coup gave a rare interview to the *Daily Telegraph* saying that he simply supported democratic regime change in Equatorial Guinea and to that end, had financed plans by Severo Moto to return to his country. 'There was a scheme to fly him back and to protect him while he was in the country. Severo's belief was that if he was protected in his home town and could remain alive for a few days a political storm would occur that would sweep away the present regime. I am not a coup planner. I don't have a talent in that sense. But yes, I financed Severo Moto's political activities and, yes, I introduced Simon Mann to him because of his background in security.' Businessman Mr X said that Mann had only himself to blame for how it all ended. 'It was his lack of professionalism, his lack of discretion, his lack of judgment that caused this situation. There was no coup plot.'

Family and friends were bitter that Mann had been left to bear the brunt of his actions pretty much on his own. Amanda's father Maurice Freedman told *The Mail on Sunday*: 'Simon went tiger shoot-ing and the tiger turned round and fought back and won the battle. He went into this thing with a sort of Boy's Own-style trust in the people he was involved with, but they've slithered away.'

In various interviews Obiang had said that Mann had provided his investors with 'valuable information about the plot on a daily basis'. The president made the startling claim that one of Mann's co-conspirators, 'Mr Big', was 'trying his best to ensure that he either kills Simon Mann in prison or kidnaps him from prison to silence him.' Because of this Obiang said, Mann had special guards in prison and his food was checked before he ate it. The conference centre location of the trial was only disclosed the night before the trial and Western journalists were told they would not be allowed into the court with shoes, long-sleeved shirts, watches or pens because 'Today, there are all sorts of sophisticated gadgets and weaponry which can easily pass undetected.' Obiang stated that his government had wanted to surround Mann with bullet-proof screens but had run out of time to install them before the trial. He said that all proper legal processes had been followed to secure Mann's extradition and vehemently denied allegations that Robert Mugabe had handed Mann over in return for cheap oil. Mann's trial, Obiang said, would be 'free, fair and transparent,' with an African Union judge, human rights groups such as Amnesty International and a British diplomat invited to be present.

Despite all these claims, there were still some dubious aspects to the trial. The week before it started, Mann's lawyer Jonathan Samkange was unceremoniously stripped of his right to practise in the country, Channel 4 was offered £50,000 to televise the proceedings (it refused) and journalists were offered the chance to buy sensitive documents that were likely to form a key part of the prosecution's case.

The BBC's West Africa correspondent, Will Ross, reported: 'Equatorial Guinea may be pleased to see the back of this trial. It has been suggested that authorities hoped the attention would provide an international boost for a country that many people struggle to find on a map. It would be cast as the victim of a greedy, arrogant, colonial-minded plot. The problem is that journalists find it difficult to cover such a story without mentioning the country's appalling human rights and corruption record, and by the time the vast oil wealth has been contrasted with the alarming poverty, the politicians running Equatorial Guinea would perhaps prefer the country to slink back into obscurity. It is a thinly disguised dictatorship. Whatever President Obiang says usually goes and so Simon Mann's best hope now is for a pardon from the very man he tried to topple.'

Another aspect of the trial was the involvement of Princess Ghida Talal, a former press secretary to the late King Hussein of Jordan and married to Prince Tala bin Muhammad, a national security adviser to Hussein and now a special adviser to King Abdullah. The

Princess arrived in Malabo because her brother, Lebanese business-man Mohamed Salaam, was in court, accused of being involved in the coup attempt. She was in Equatorial Guinea with her sister Dalia and mother Rajaa. On 8 July, the *Guardian* reported: 'Sources close to the family say the princess has been allowed personally to plead for clemency with the president, Teodoro Obiang Nguema, through the offices of the King of Morocco, who provides Obiang with his special bodyguard ... Mohamed's father, Hany, is a friend and business partner of the anonymous businessman, alleged to be the main backer of the coup. He has denied the allegation.'

During the trial, Mohamed said that he had met Mann who had presented him with a proposal for a fisheries protection project – Mann's advance mercenary party had set up a fishing business in Malabo as a front activity – and that he had no idea the project was a cover. When Mann was extradited to Equatorial Guinea, Mohamed's name was included amongst those who had had a peripheral role in the plot and he was arrested after Simon Mann was extradited from Zimbabwe. Salaam had based himself full-time in Equatorial Guinea since 2001 and was said at one time to have received a gift of around $25,000 from Obiang for 'services to the country' but had then fallen out of favour. Like all the other arrested alleged conspirators, Salaam had a very anxious family. Said his father: 'I am extremely worried about my son's health. Mohamed has suffered from bouts of malaria which triggered two bipolar breakdowns. He has suffered a third breakdown which could be very damaging to his permanent mental health.' During Salaam's testimony the electricity failed and he proceedings had to continue without microphones or air conditioning. Shortly before the trial began, Mohammed had angrily interrupted Mann when he told reporters they were being treated well, shouting: 'Simon, stop lying about how we are. Just stop it.'

On 7 July 2008, Mann was found guilty in a heavily-guarded court of attempting to buy arms for an alleged coup and his 'abortive mercenary coup attempt' and sentenced to thirty-four years in jail. He was also ordered to pay a fine and compensation to the Equatorial State of around $24m. During the trial, Jose Olo Obano, Equatorial Guinea's attorney general, had urged the court to sentence Mann to thirty-one years, eight months and three days. Fortunately for Mann, however, the death penalty was not permitted under the terms of his extradition from Zimbabwe. Wearing a grey prison uniform,

Mann stood impassively as the sentence was read out by presiding judge Carlo Mangue who said that despite his apology to the court, Mann had not shown 'an attitude of regret', and that the sentence was justified because of the 'seriousness of the crimes' and the weight of evidence. Asked if he had a message for his family, Mann said: 'I love you – and chin up.'

But Mann admitted: 'It was a fuck-up. I blame myself for not simply saying "cut". I was bloody stupid. I regret all that terribly. You go tiger shooting and you don't expect the tiger to win. I have been saying how sorry I am to everybody for four years now actually ... I thought there was quite a good chance I was going to die, because I knew that far too many people knew about the operation.'

Despite his sister's intervention Mohamed Salaam received an eighteen-year prison sentence. Four Equatorial Guinea nationals received prison terms of six years each and another was jailed for a year.

Out of the original seventy accused men, sixty-four were acquitted.

Obiang announced that if the British police 'arrest the people we say were also involved – Mr X, Mark Thatcher and the others, then maybe we will transfer Simon to an English jail so he can be close to his family.'

Writing on internet site Head Heritage, one observer of the Mann debacle was scathing about news coverage of his plight. Said Julian Cope: 'Isn't it odd how whenever someone British is tried abroad the media always take their side. Always, this insinuation that it's a miscarriage of justice, some terrible travesty, cos surely our people are good, and anyway no other country is grown-up enough to have a proper legal system, not like our faultless one here ... Simon Mann was described in the British press as "looking more like a jailed intellectual than a freelance commando." What is there in a mercenary leader's appearance that would be so different from a jailed intellectual? As Leonard Cohen said in response to the normality of the captured Nazi Adolf Eichmann, "what did you expect? Talons? Oversize incisors? Green saliva?" ... A humane and romantic breaker of both British law and the Geneva Convention, Mann is an ex-SAS soldier who runs a company called Executive Outcomes. They are mercenary soldiers, using apartheid South Africa's special forces for butchering whoever they are paid to. The phrase "international terrorist" could not be more aptly applied.

The quote from a friend saying he and his companies have "been scrupulous about operating in concert with Western policy goals" is right on the money though. Him and his mercenary scum friends have been making sure the rich get richer by fucking over the poor and the environment, a clear Western policy goal if ever there was one. They've exacerbated wars in order to get themselves personal wealth not only by providing the troops, but by taking the mineral resources of the lands they're fighting in.'

Mann was convinced he would die in the hellish Black Beach prison in Malabo. Situated on the tropical volcanic island of Bioko, it has been described as a 'black hole' into which prisoners simply disappear. Food rations, already meagre, were reduced even more; visits from legal representatives denied. Horror stories abounded about brutality and the mysterious disappearance of those incarcerated there. Human rights organisation Amnesty knows all about Black Beach. Said Kolawole Olaniyan, director of its Africa programme: 'Many prisoners are extremely weak because of torture or ill-treatment and chronic illness. Unless immediate action is taken, many of those detained there will die. It is a scandalous failure by the authorities to fulfil their most basic responsibilities under international law.' Another Amnesty campaign director, Stephen Bowen, added: 'Such near starvation, lack of medical attention and appalling prison conditions are nothing short of a slow, lingering death sentence.'

On 16 July 2008, Amnesty International issued a press release, outlining its concerns over the arrests and trial of the accused men.

Equatorial Guinea: Concerns about the recent trial of Simon Mann and other co-accused

On 7 July 2008, eight people – including six Equatorial Guineans and two foreign nationals – were sentenced to long prison terms in Equatorial Guinea after a trial that failed to comply with international standards of fair trials.

Simon Mann, a British citizen, was convicted of attempting to commit crimes against the Head of State, crimes against the government, and crimes against the peace and independence of Equatorial Guinea in 2004. He was sentenced to a total of 34 years imprisonment. Simon Mann was released from prison in

Zimbabwe in May 2007 after completing a sentence for trying to buy arms without a licence, and was immediately arrested pending his extradition to Equatorial Guinea to face the above charges.

Mohamed Salaam, a Lebanese businessman resident in Equatorial Guinea for several years, was convicted of the same offences and sentenced to 18 years in prison. He was arrested without a warrant on 29 March 2008.

Six Equatorial Guineans who were arrested without a warrant in March and April 2008 (see Equatorial Guinea: Arrests and death in custody of a political opponent [AI Index: AFR 24/003/2008]) were also tried in the same trial. They were charged and convicted of illegal association, for being members of the banned Progress Party of Equatorial Guinea (*Partido del Progreso de Guinea Ecuatorial* – PPGE) and holding meetings in early 2006, and for possession of arms and ammunition. Cruz Obiang Ebele, Emiliano Esono Michá, Gerardo Angüe Mangue, Gumersindo Ramírez Faustino, and Juan Ecomo Ndong were sentenced to six years in prison, while Bonifácio Nguema Ndong received a prison term of one year.

Amnesty International is concerned that the six Equatorial Guineans were tried in the same trial as Simon Mann, who was tried for an alleged coup attempt in March 2004, despite the fact that the charges against them were not related to the events for which Simon Mann was tried. According to the information received by Amnesty International, no attempt was made in court to link the six Equatorial Guineans to Simon Mann's case, nor was any evidence produced to that effect.

Amnesty International is also concerned that the six Equatorial Guineans may be prisoners of conscience arrested solely for peacefully exercising their right to freedom of association and assembly, and convicted on the basis of statements they signed under duress and/or under torture.

Amnesty International is further concerned about aspects of the pre-trial stage that violated the right to a fair trial. In particular, Amnesty International is concerned that:

- The six Equatorial Guineans and Mohamed Salaam were arrested without a warrant in contravention of Equatorial Guinean law and their right not to be arbitrarily arrested.

- At least with regard to the Equatorial Guineans, they were not promptly informed of the charges against them and were only informed a couple of months after their arrest.
- The Equatorial Guineans gave their statements under duress. Their statements were not taken by the *juez de Instrucción*, (investigating judge) as prescribed by Equatorial Guinea law. The accused saw the investigating judge for the first time on 12 June 2008, when he read out the charges against them. They gave their statements first to the police and then to the Prosecutor in the presence of the Minister of National Security but without any legal representation in violation of their right to communicate with a lawyer. In addition, contrary to the provisions of international human rights standards of fair trial that no one may be compelled to confess guilt or testify against themselves, they were forced to sign statements they had not made.
- At least two of the Equatorial Guineans were subjected to cruel, inhuman and degrading treatment by being beaten while in police custody.
- The defendants were held incommunicado in Black Beach prison in Malabo, without access either to their families or to their lawyer. This had a negative impact on the physical and mental health of the defendants, particularly on Mohamed Salaam. Incommunicado detention infringes international human rights standards of fair trial that guarantee all detained persons the right of access to family, a doctor and a lawyer.
- In violation of international human rights standard of fair trial, the defendants did not get adequate time or facilities to prepare their defence. They did not have access to a lawyer until five days before the start of the trial, and they did not have access to all the relevant information needed to prepare their defence.

Amnesty International is also concerned about some aspects of the trial itself. In particular, the organization is concerned that:

- In court, the Equatorial Guineans retracted their statements on the basis that they were made under duress and torture. However, the court did not examine the allegations of coercion and allowed the statements to be admitted as evidence. Furthermore, in the summing up at the end of the trial the Attorney General requested an additional 20 years to be added to their sentence for failing to

107

collaborate with the administration of justice by stating in court that they had been forced to sign statements under duress.

- The six Equatorial Guineans were convicted of holding illegal meetings and being members of a banned political party in violation of their rights to freedom of association and assembly. Furthermore, the prosecution failed to produce evidence that they were in fact in possession of arms or ammunition thereby failing to discharge the burden of proof. The prosecutor was unable to prove beyond reasonable doubt that the accused were guilty. By convicting the accused when the standard of proof was not met, the court violated their right to a fair trial.
- Interpretation was provided only for the part of the trial which directly related to the questioning of Simon Mann and Mohamed Salaam. Other parts of the trial, including the reading of the indictment were conducted in Spanish. Consequently, the two men were not able to follow the whole proceedings, in violation of their right to equality of arms.
- On the first day of the trial, Simon Mann entered the court room with shackles on his feet. Although the presiding officer promptly ordered them to be removed, this constituted cruel, inhuman and degrading treatment and impinged on the presumption of innocence.

Amnesty International is concerned about the reported state of mental health of Mohamed Salaam and calls on the Equatorial Guinean authorities to fulfil their international human rights obligations and grant him immediate access to appropriate medical treatment.

The organization calls on the Equatorial Guinean authorities to respect the right to fair trial and comply with their international human rights obligations. In particular, Amnesty International calls for the allegations of torture and ill-treatment to be investigated and for those suspected of involvement in these allegations to be brought to justice. In addition the authorities should grant all prisoners immediate access to their families, lawyers and any medical treatment they may require.

In an interview with the *Daily Mail* Amanda Mann spoke of her fears about her husband being incarcerated in Black Beach prison, saying: 'It was like a dagger to my heart when I heard he was there.

One of the things that fills me with fear is they will beat the living daylights out of him. That could be happening as I speak. Or that there will be one of those "accidents" that happen in these places.' In another interview, she said: 'I shake with fear of the day I have to tell my children that Simon won't be coming home' and castigated Thatcher and other coup associates for not offering their support, saying: 'I'm hurt because I think what goes around comes around.'

President Obiang went on record to say the prison had greatly improved in recent years and was now 'the best prisons in the whole of Africa . . . like a five-star hotel.' This had not always been the case. A human rights report stated that at one time Black Beach officials had stopped providing seventy prisoners with meals and blocked all contact with families, lawyers and consular officials and were 'in danger of death due to starvation and torture.' It was also reported that prisoners were kept in their cells for twenty-four hours a day and that foreign detainees were held with their hands and legs 'cuffed at all times.' Obiang denied the allegations on national radio, saying that the prisoners were well treated. He also denied that male prisoners sexually assaulted female ones and that prisoners were used as unpaid workers on construction projects for certain government officials.

Having spent time in prison Mann maintained he was 'not the person I was.' But he also still maintained that Spain and South Africa, with the endorsement of South African president Thabo Mbeki, had supported the coup plans and that by January 2004 the mission was 'like an official operation. The government of Spain and South Africa were giving the green light "You've got to go. You've got to do it."' The South African government issued a public denial of supporting Mann in any way, saying: 'South Africa will never, tacitly or expressly, support the use of mercenaries to bring about fundamental political changes in an country in our continent or elsewhere in the world including Equatorial Guinea. Simon Mann and his ilk must fully understand that the days of military coups are indeed over and those implicated in such activities will indeed face the full might of the laws of the countries of our continent.'

Mann further added that he 'regretted' what had happened and that 'It was wrong and I'm happy we did not succeed.' Mann said he was 'extremely grateful' not only for the pardon 'but for the way in which I've been treated from the moment I arrived here in Equatorial Guinea in 2008.

On 3 September 2008, 64-year-old Severo Moto gave an exclusive interview to the *Daily Telegraph* in which he admitted hiring Simon Mann for the Equatorial Guinea coup. He said the two men had met on several occasions in his exiled home of Madrid and that an agreement was struck for Mann to provide protection so he could return to Equatorial Guinea and 'fight for democratic change' adding: 'It would be impossible to survive there without protection of some sort. Simon offered it.' Moto also expressed his sorrow that Mann was now in jail, saying: 'I feel very bad about Simon ending up in prison there. It is one of the worst places in the world and is the path of death' but he added: 'He had taken on the role of protecting me in that place so he fully knew the risks involved. What has been done to him while he is there is down to the regime, not me.' Moto said Mann had been duped into giving evidence at his trial on the understanding that he would be treated leniently. 'He collaborated and gave them the names they wanted to hear clearly in the hope that they may reward him. He fell into temptation and can't be blamed for that but I know those people and there will be no leniency, no pardon. He can only hope they don't kill him.'

Moto said that he had received financial backing from the businessman (which he had admitted), but he denied knowing Mark Thatcher was involved in the attempted coup. Moto also used the interview to accuse Western countries of collaborating with Equatorial Guinea's repressive regime in return for oil contracts and called on them to help overthrow the country instead, saying that although his party had won elections in Equatorial Guinea, president Obiang would not permit opposition.

Moto further claimed that Spain had colluded with Equatorial Guinea by revoking his asylum status in 2005 and threatening to send him back from which he had been exiled.

This whole saga was indeed one of political intrigue.

Chapter 10

A Country in need of Conquering

So just where and what is the country that Simon Mann and his co-plotters wanted to 'invade'?

With the full name The Republic of Equatorial Guinea, It is a small country (about 10,830 square miles) squeezed in between Cameroon and Gabon off West Africa and home to a population of around 676,000. Equatorial Guinea is composed of a small chunk of the African mainland – Rio Muni – and a collection of five islands including Corisco and Elobey. Its capital, Malabo (formerly Santa Isabel) is situated on the island of Bioko, formerly known as Fernando Po, the name of the man who discovered it.

Mainland Río Muni dominates in size but generally has not dominated in economical matters. In history, the focus for colonialists was the island of Bioko until the year 2000. Since independence in 1968, the mainland has played a more significant role, mostly due to the Rio Muni origins of the two presidents.

The climate is humid and tropical. Soil on the mainland is poor meaning agriculture has always been small-scale – mostly 'slash and burn'. Hunting and gathering have therefore always had an important role. Dominated by rain forests and with agricultural conditions promoting semi-sedentary communities, population density is low. On Bioko, soils are somewhat richer due to the volcanic nature of the island, but heavy rains on most of the island, and a hilly landscape, restrict agriculture to just a few areas.

Two peoples inhabit the regions of Equatorial Guinea, the Bubi and the Fang. The Bubi live on Bioko and were probably the first to settle on the island. The Bubi population originally succeeded in isolating itself from arriving foreigners and even when the first cocoa plantations were established, Europeans brought slaves and contract workers from the West African continent. Through centuries of interaction of Bubi, Europeans and West African imported labour, a Creole population emerged – the Fernandinos. The Fang is the dominant people of the Río Muni mainland and boasts the highest number. Fang also populate vast areas in Cameroon and Gabon. The Fang people, however, have not lived for long in the rainforest climate of Southern Cameroon, Equatorial Guinea and Northern Gabon. Until the political instability in Central Cameroon in the mid-nineteenth century, it is believed that the Fang lived in these northern areas, between the savannah and the rainforest. They conquered the sparsely populated areas were they are now settled from the Ndowe and other Bantu peoples (related to the Fang). The Ndowe themselves, are believed to have won the land from the Pygmies living there originally during the Bantu expansion. Ndowe are still a relatively important people in several zones of Río Muni but are out-numbered by the Fang.

The major languages are Spanish and French; the main religion is Christianity. The country was initially discovered by Portuguese explorer, Fernando Po, in 1471 and remained in Portugal control until Spain received the territory in 1778. In earlier years contract workers were recruited from Liberia and then from Nigeria. The Bubis were a minor part of the working force and most worked on the plantations as forced labour. It was only in the final years of colonialism that Bubis were involved much more in cocoa production as several village co-operatives had been established. Other industries on Bioko included some production of coffee and some livestock. Spain continued to be the primary influence until pressure was put on the country to give the colony its independence in the 1950s and 1960s. This pressure was particularly strong from the United Nations, especially the Afro-Asian group, and from a small circle of people within the colony. The colony was made autonomous in 1964, meaning independence in economical matters, but with a Spanish right of veto in decision-making. A legislative power was established and the Fang politician Bonifacio Ondo Edu was elected president of the Executive Council. The constitution of 1967 led Spanish Guinea towards independence after nearly 200 years of Spanish rule and foresaw a strong presidential power. It also

112

hoped to prepare the way for democracy. Presidential elections in autumn 1968 gave victory to the Fang Francisco Macias Nguema, an opportunistic clerk from Mongomo with Spanish, military training.

Today, Equatorial Guinea has one of the worst human rights reputations on the continent.

So, Francisco Macias Nguema became the first elected president of Equatorial Guinea. This was the only legitimate election this country would experience for the next forty years. But it heralded a bloody and brutal regime with the country being nicknamed 'the Dachau of Africa' and Nguema ordering political executions. Nguema won most votes in rural Rio Muni with his promise to return 'traditional' Fang values and threats to take over European businesses. The educated Fang and the Bubi distanced themselves from Nguema and mainly voted for the other candidate, Equatorial Guinea's pre-independence Prime Minister Bonifacio Ondu Edu. It was these groups who were to become the focus of most of the persecution by Nguema's dictatorship. Equatorial Guinea was proclaimed an independent republic in October 1968, and Nguema took office as its president. Fearing reprisals, Ondu had fled to Gabon but was forced back to Equatorial Guinea where he was executed in January 1969 – the year that persecution of politicians from the opposition started in earnest. A few months later Nguema killed an opponent by breaking his legs and letting him die of malnutrition. He then murdered ten members of his Cabinet. Other officials, including a former vice-president 'committed suicide' while in detention. Political murders became the order of everyday. At the same time, attacks started on Spanish citizens, leading to an evacuation of most Europeans (about 7,500 Spanish) by the Spanish government. In 1970, all opposition was prohibited.

On 7 May 1971, Nguema issued 'Decree 415' which repealed parts of the 1968 Constitution and granted him 'all direct powers of Government and Institutions' including powers formerly held by the legislative and judiciary branches, as well as the cabinet of ministers. On 18 October 1971, 'Law 1' was issued which imposed the death penalty as punishment for threatening the President or the government. Insulting or offending the President or his cabinet was punishable by thirty years in prison. On 14 July 1972, Nguema declared himself President for Life with 'Constitutional Decree 1'. He completely repealed the 1968 Constitution on 29 July 1973, instituting a new Constitution that gave him and his party absolute power. Nguema declared private education 'subversive' and banned it entirely with 'Decree 6' on 18 March 1975. During Nguema's regime, the country had absolutely no plans for development and there was no system in place to deal with public funds. (Nguema had killed the governor of the Central Bank and took all money that was still left in the national treasury to his village home.) During the Christmas of 1975 he ordered the deaths of about 150 of his opponents. They were executed by soldiers who shot them at the football stadium in the capital town of Malabo, while amplifiers were playing Mary Hopkin's *Those were the Days*.

Nguema created three 'political parties' during his reign: the United National Workers' Party (PUNT, which he formed to replace the pre-independence parties), the *Juventud en Marcha con Macías* militia/youth group, and the Esangui clan of Río Muni. The repression suffered by the people was entirely controlled by Nguema's relatives and followers who were enrolled in a variety of positions including in the military and his bodyguard. Nguema was unpredictable, paranoid and irrational – he banned the use of the word 'intellectual', emptied schools, minimalised healthcare – he banned medicines, which led to the widespread return of tropical diseases including yellow fever, malaria, leprosy, diphtheria, typhus and cholera – and let water and electricity supplies diminish. People were tortured, killed, exiled, and imprisoned for wearing a pair of glasses. Prisoners at Black Beach jail were ritualistically held to the floor, as their skulls were crushed with iron bars by other prisoners.

Nguema 'Africanized' his name to Masie Nguema Biyogo Ñegue Ndong in 1976 after demanding that the rest of the Equatoguinean population do the same. (The island of Fernando Pò had its name 'Africanized' after him to Masie Nguema Biyogo Island but following his removal it was re-named Bioko.) Nguema also called himself 'Unique Miracle' and 'Grand Master of Education, Science and Culture'. Nguema allegedly committed genocide against the Bubi ethnic minority, ordered the death of thousands of suspected opponents, closed down churches and was overseer of the collapse of the economy.

By 1973, a quarter of the Equatorial Guinean population had left. Almost the entire intellectual, political and economical groups had fled or been killed. Almost every key post in the civil administration and the military was given to Nguema's relatives.

Threats and physical attacks on Nigerian contract workers by government forces led to the Nigerian evacuation of all its citizens from Equatorial Guinea in 1976. These 25,000 workers were the key stone in the countries export industries, as they were the only one competent to manage the cocoa plantations.

Most cocoa plantations, including the village cooperatives, were nationalised. But the most devastating effect on the economy was the evacuation of the Nigerian workers. The steadily deteriorating relationship with foreign businesses also saw outside investments in cocoa decline. The country had now lost its main industry. Other industries, such as the coffee and oil palm production, livestock and logging, met the same fate. The Bubi people, which still preferred a livelihood outside the plantations, were now forcefully recruited to replace the Nigerians on the badly managed state farms.

The presidential decree commanding obligatory forced labour on plantations, under inhumane working conditions, made refugee streams out of Equatorial Guinea increase even more. To hinder the exodus from Bioko, the president ordered all boats and ship, not regarding their size, to be destroyed (although this led to the total closure of the lucrative fishing industry). The national economy totally collapsed.

By 1979 Nguema's violations of human rights during his reign had caused more than a third of the country's population to flee.

Frank Ruddy, US ambassador to Equatorial Guinea under President Reagan, said: 'It's a corrupt, rotten government'.

On 3 August 1979 Nguema was overthrown in a bloody coup led by his nephew Teodoro Obiang Nguema, the young lieutenant colonel in charge of Black Beach prison and previously the military governor of Bioko and Vice-Minister of the Armed Forces. Obiang, a Fang, had studied at the Spanish Military Academy in Zaragoza just as his uncle had done. His relationship to the first president of Equatorial Guinea had seen a meteoric rise in his career (something enjoyed by many or Nguema's other relatives). His position of governor had given him incredible power as Nguema, by this time, was a virtual recluse, living in a bunker. Fears that he might be an assassination target had seen him murdering more and more of his own family members. In June 1979, Obiang heard that his brother had been killed by Nguema's bodyguards and surviving family members wondered who was next. Obiang took the initiative to gather together various nephews and cousins who had graduated from Zaragoza and to start planning a coup. He was in an excellent position to do so and even obtained the support from the Spanish government, which had given up on Nguema. Although Nguema and a contingent of loyal forces tried to resist the coup, his forces eventually abandoned him and Bioko and Bata were quickly taken. Obiang was captured in a forest on 18 August – reportedly with the country's entire foreign currency reserves – £100m – stuffed into suitcases.

That same day the Supreme Military Council opened 'Case 1/979' and started interviewing witnesses and collecting evidence against the Macías Nguema regime. The Council subsequently convened a military tribunal on 24 September to try Nguema and several members of his regime. The charges for the ten defendants included genocide, mass murder, embezzlement of public funds, violations of human rights, and treason.

The state prosecutor requested that Nguema should face the death penalty, that five of his allies should each be sentenced to thirty years in prison and another four each sentenced to a year in prison. Nguema's defence council argued that the co-defendants were responsible for specific crimes, and asked for acquittal. Nguema himself delivered a statement to the court outlining what he viewed as the good work he had done for his country. At noon on 29 September 1979, the Tribunal delivered its sentences – which were more severe than had been requested. Nguema and six of his co-defendants were sentenced to death – Nguema 'a hundred and one times' – with the order that their property should be confiscated. Two defendants were sentenced to fourteen years in prison, and two others to four years.

With no allowance in Equatorial Guinea's legal system to appeal the sentences were final. Nguema and the six other men were executed by a Moroccan firing squad at Black Beach prison at 6pm on the same day.

Nguema left behind him the reputation as one of the most klepto-cratic, corrupt and dictatorial leaders in post-colonial African history. He has been compared to Pol Pot, the leader of the Cambodian Communist movement known as the Khmer Rouge and Prime

Minister of Democratic Kampuchea for three years until 1979. During that time Pol Pot 'cleansed' the country resulting in the deaths of up to two and a half million people. Both regimes were violent, unpredictable and anti-intellectual.

The 1982 constitution of Equatorial Guinea gives any President extensive powers including naming and dismissing members of the cabinet, making laws by decree, dissolving the Chamber of Representatives, negotiating and ratifying treaties and calling legislative elections. The President retains his role as commander in chief of the armed forces and minister of defence, and he maintains close supervision of the military activity.

In 1995, America's President Bill Clinton closed the American embassy in the country. President George Bush renewed diplomatic relations in 2001 and in October 2003 the embassy was re-opened, staffed by one officer assisted by other embassy officials resident in Cameroon – and housed in property rented from the Equatorial Guinea's National Security Minister Manuel Nguema Mba – who has constantly been linked to abuse of human rights. On a tour of Africa, Bush made a point of visiting president Obiang. It was reported that Bush felt 'intense lobbying' to re-open the American embassy in Equatorial Guinea and that he had received a memo from the oil industry which read: 'It is important to underscore that most of the oil and gas concessions awarded in Equatorial Guinea to date have been awarded to US firms. This is in stark contrast to neighboring countries in the region, where the United States has consistently lost out to French and other European and Asian competitors.'

Differences between the Fang and the Bubi have been a major source of political tension over the years, often erupting into violence. On 21 January 1998, Bubis led a separatist revolt on Bioko, after which the Fang-dominated government stepped up its repression of the Bubis, allowing Fang vigilante groups a free hand.

Obiang is currently Africa's second longest-serving leader after Libya's Muammar Gaddafi, having been in power for over thirty years. The people of Equatorial Guinea may have felt they were in more compassionate hands when Obiang relaxed some aspects of his predecessor's regime such as the ban on the Catholic Church, but the desire for total power and oppression of any opponents was the same. So too was the corruption.

117

Officially Obiang won more than ninety-seven per cent in the presidential elections in December 2002. But opposition candidates had withdrawn claiming fraud and 'irregularities'. This did not stop state radio declaring Obiang to be 'in permanent contact with the Almighty' or an aid describing him as 'like God in Heaven', adding: 'He can decide to kill without anyone calling him to account and without going to hell because it is God himself with whom he is in permanent contact and who gives him this strength.'

An Amnesty International report simply concluded: 'There have been no free, fair, and transparent elections since independence in 1968. The international community criticized the 2004 parliamentary elections as seriously flawed. Prior to elections the government harassed opposition party members and subjected them to arbitrary arrest. PDGE (the country's Democratic Party) members went door-to-door, seeking out and threatening opposition supporters. PDGE party posters appeared in public places, including churches. On election day there were widespread reports of irregularities, including intimidation at the polls. Voters were discouraged from voting in secret, ballots were opened, and ruling party representatives reportedly cast their own votes as well as those of children and the deceased. There also were reports that security forces intimidated voters with their presence in polling booths. There was a lack of observers in rural areas. Although international observers claimed that the opposition CPDS (Convergence for Social Democracy) party received about 12 per cent of the vote, the ruling party offered the CPDS only 2 seats in the 100-seat parliament.'

But despite the poverty, corruption and deprivation of the country – with no electricity, sewage running through the streets, no fresh water, a life expectancy of just fifty-four – and the brutal rule, Equatorial Guinea attracted little attention, from human rights groups or others, until it had something which the world wanted.

A modest oilfield was discovered in its territorial waters in the Gulf of Guinea which went on to produce 17,000 barrels of crude oil a day. This was insignificant compared to other countries, but enough to warrant further investigation. In 1995 Exxon Mobil discovered a huge new oil field off Bioko island. Around twenty companies were later to ask for drilling rights. Today, the Gulf of Guinea's oil reserves, which are owned by several countries, are estimated at more than one billion barrels, as much as ten per cent of the world's total. In 2004 the oil fields were producing 360 barrels a day, accounting for ninety per cent of the country's exports. Obiang found himself being feted with American oil tycoons flying in to make his acquaintance. They wanted his oil but found it hard to stomach his way of ruling. 'This is the sh**hole of the planet. Our bosses hate the corruption, they hate these guys, and most of all they hate the protocol,' one oil executive told *Spiegel Online International*.

But today most of the world's largest oil companies now trade with Equatorial Guinea, including Amerada Hess, ChevronTexaco, Devon Energy, Energy Africa, Marathon, Noble Affiliates and Petronas. Firms involved in oil exploration there include Chevron, ExxonMobil, Vanco, Atlas and Devon, all based in the United States; Roc, based in Australia; Petronas, based in Malaysia; South Africa's Sasol; Britain's Noble; and Glencore, based in Switzerland.

At times, the oil industry has tried to reduce the control the Equatorial Guinea government has over hiring people in the industry and to 'eliminate political bias'. To this end companies advertised jobs publicly and screened all applications – all to little result. It was made clear that employment and security agencies controlled largely by Obiang's relatives should be used instead.

A vast natural gas field also was discovered and Equatorial Guinea signed a $1.4 billion deal with Houston-based Marathon Oil to construct a liquefied natural gas facility on Bioko. British Gas signed a seventeen-year agreement to buy products from the facility.

In 2004 a US Senate investigation into the Washington-based Riggs Bank found that Obiang's family had received huge payments from American oil companies including ExxonMobil and Amerada Hess. It was said that ExxonMobil had given Obiang a stake in an oil-trading business for just $2,300. Six years later, Obiang's holding was valued at around $645,000. Exxon and Amerada Hess paid around $1m to Sonavi, a private security firm headed by Obiang's brother Armengol Ondo Nguema (the country's security chief and identified in State Department reports as a torturer). Amerada Hess also paid government officials and their relatives more than $2m for building and office leases. About a quarter of this was paid to Obiang's 14-year-old son. In all, it was estimated that around $700m was deposited for the Equatorial Guinea government and Obiang's relatives. Using wire transfers some $35m was drained from an account that held oil revenues for the country's people and put into offshore accounts. Riggs was fined £25m for a 'wilful, systematic' violation of anti-money laundering laws. One Riggs employee, Simon P. Kareri, who dealt with Equatorial Guinea, was reported to return from the country with suitcases stuffed with millions of dollars.

It was said that the companies were pulling out all the stops to win favour with and contracts from, Obiang and his coterie. The report concluded: 'Oil companies operating in Equatorial Guinea may have contributed to corrupt practices in that country by making substantial payments to, or entering into business ventures with, individual Equatorial Guinea officials, their family members, or entities they control, with minimal public disclosure of their actions.'

That same year a report by the US Department of Energy concluded: 'There is strong evidence that oil revenues have been misappropriated by the government. Furthermore, the government's failure to direct oil revenues toward development – especially to fund urgently needed infrastructure improvements – has undermined economic and social progress in the country.'

As a result of the energy finds, the nation has become the third largest recipient of direct investment from US firms in sub-Saharan Africa. The international investment has raised Equatorial Guinea's per capita annual income from $370 in 1995 to nearly $10,000 today. According to the International Monetary Fund (IMF), its income from oil and gas is about one billion pounds a year but it is likely to be three times this amount. It is believed that within five years the country will probably be Africa's second biggest producer and one of America's largest providers. Obiang is unforthcoming about his country's true fortunes. In 1998 he claimed he was paid $34m in oil royalties when the IMF declared it to be $130m. (In 2008 the country was included in an international initiative for countries to be more open about oil reserves but failed to meet the requested April 2010 deadline.)

Yet seventy per cent of the population is malnourished and eight in ten of its people struggle to survive. The United Nations says that less than half the population has access to clean drinking water and that twenty per cent of children die before reaching the age of five. President Obiang and his family misappropriate much of the country's income. He and his predecessor have been described as among the worst abusers of human rights in the whole of Africa.

Transparency International has put Equatorial Guinea in the top twelve of its most corrupt states.

But business between Equatorial Guinea and other countries continues. On 2 June 2005, the *Guardian* reported that BG Plc, formerly British Gas, was taking full-page 'prestige advertisements in *New Statesman*, the Labour magazine, to boast that it intends to "play an important role in securing Britain's energy supply." The company says it hopes to make considerable profits on what is being touted as the fuel of the future. It is buying up nearly 60 million tonnes of liquefied natural gas – the entire planned output for 17 years of Equatorial Guinea's new LNG plant – an amount that is worth about $15 billion at today's prices ... The financial relationships are opaque. John Haden, from Worcestershire, Incat's owner, said he would not reveal the extent of GEPetrol's planned shareholding ... Asked about the problem of corruption in Equatorial Guinea, Mr Haden said: "Yes, but what about the rest of Africa?"'

The report added that the campaigning organisation Global Witness wanted UK firms to take more responsibility for the 'oil curse' that Equatorial Guinea suffers. It quoted Global Witness's special analyst Sarah Wykes: 'American oil companies have been accused of activities at best morally questionable and, at worst, corrupt and illegal. Given the EG government's history of corruption, and the controversial track record of other extractive sector companies operating there, it is in the interests both of its citizens and of BG, that the company break this pattern and disclose fully what it is paying to the EG government for its gas.'

The response from BG was: 'We are founding signatories of the transparency initiative. But in this case we are not dealing with the EG government. We are dealing with a private entity, in a commercially confidential contract.'

In 2006, the Bureau of Democracy, Human Rights and Labor, produced a report about Equatorial Guinea. It said that the government's human rights record was 'poor' and that the government 'continued to commit or condone serious abuses.' It listed the following 'human rights problems':

- *Abridgement of citizens' right to change their government*
- *Security force torture, beating, and other physical abuse of prisoners and detainees*

- *Harsh and life-threatening prison conditions*
- *Impunity*
- *Arbitrary arrest, detention, and incommunicado detention*
- *Harassment, detention, and deportation of foreign residents*
- *Judicial corruption and lack of due process*
- *Restrictions on the right of privacy*
- *Severe restrictions on freedom of speech and of the press*
- *Restrictions on the rights of assembly, association, and movement*
- *Government corruption*
- *Restrictions on human rights nongovernmental organizations (NGOs)*
- *Violence and discrimination against women*
- *Trafficking in persons*
- *Discrimination against ethnic minorities and HIV/AID victims*
- *Restrictions on labour rights*
- *Forced labour*
- *Child labour*

The report said that although the government 'or its agents' did not commit politically-motivated killings, security forces 'reportedly killed several persons through abuse and excessive force.'

It stated that there were 'continuing reports of government figures hiring persons in foreign countries to intimidate, threaten and even assassinate citizens in exile' – this included Severo Moto, exiled in Spain.

No action was ever taken against killings – such as soldiers slaughtering between twelve and sixteen people suspected of plotting a coup attempt in 2004, or the killing of a Spanish aid worker in 2003.

Added the report: 'The government did not prosecute any members of the security forces considered responsible for unlawful killings in previous years, nor was it likely to do so.'

An Amnesty International report also listed a catalogue of disappearances and 'politically-motivated kidnappings' and commented on 'torture and other cruel, inhuman or degrading treatment or punishment' in Equatorial Guinea, saying: 'The law does not specifically prohibit such practices, and although the law mandates respect for the liberty and dignity of persons and adherence to the Universal Declaration on Human Rights, members of the security forces tortured, beat, and otherwise abused suspects, prisoners, and opposition politicians ... it was reported that torture was widespread in the country's places of detention and during the course of trials. In 2004 senior government officials told foreign diplomats that human rights did not apply to criminals and that torture of known criminals was not a human rights abuse. No action has been taken, or is expected to be taken against security forces responsible for torture.'

In September 2005 Amnesty International reported that navy Commandant Juan Ondo Abaga, former Lieutenant Colonel Florencio Ela Bibang, Felipe Esonoa Ntumu 'Pancho' and Antimo Edu had all simply disappeared. Abaga, a refugee resident in Benin, was allegedly abducted by Equatorial Guinean personnel and taken to Black Beach prison where he was reportedly tortured. Bibang and Ntumu had fled the country in October 2004 and were arrested in Lagos, Nigeria, with Edu. Security personnel then transported them to Black Beach prison in Equatorial Guinea where they were allegedly tortured. When asked about them, government officials claimed to have no record of the prisoners – who were reported to be held in an old part of the prison.

Around seventy people charged with offences related to another alleged coup attempt in October 2004 were reportedly tortured before and during their 'questionable secret military' trial. 'All but two of the defendants reportedly stated in court that they had been tortured in detention and some reportedly still bore visible marks. One man apparently had to be carried in and out of court as he was still unable to walk. One woman reportedly suffered from vaginal bleeding as a result of torture. It was reported that statements were extracted by torture during incommunicado detention at Bata Prison and used as evidence.' The report listed a number of names of those who had dared to challenge Obiang's rule and who had suffered for it.

Legend has it that Obiang eats the testicles of his defeated enemies so that he can absorb their life force.

The report also contained details of police corruption and violence, harassment of foreigners from other countries and rape.

Even oil company employees who were helping finance Obiang's lifestyle were stopped at checkpoints and had bribes demanded from them. The report added: 'Corruption was endemic within the security forces. Citizens who were not police officers were allowed to arrest persons suspected of being illegal residents, increasing the frequency of arbitrary arrests based on xenophobia. Members of the security forces were rarely held accountable for abuses; impunity for police officers and gendarmes was a serious problem. There are no mechanisms to investigate allegations of police abuse. The police are misused by other ministries to harass and threaten persons and to confiscate property, instead of those ministries pursuing proper legal recourse for supposed infractions.'

Diplomats and even ministers have been caught smuggling drugs. One minister was arrested in Spain in 1997 for drug trafficking. He wrote a confession in which he alleged that drugs had been distributed in Europe using diplomatic bags and even Obiang's luggage on state trips.

Arrests without proper reason are rife in Equatorial Guinea: 'There continued to be reports that security forces regularly searched homes and arrested occupants without warrants, generally with impunity. After making arrests, security personnel regularly looted homes, confiscated cars, and had family members evicted. After their release, arrested persons had no recourse for recovery of property and were often blacklisted from employment opportunities, reportedly under orders from members of the president's family.'

A report from *International Viewpoint* commented: 'The corrupt, regressive regime of President Obiang has survived frequent coup attempts. The failed coup attempt in March 2004 is not likely to be the last to decide who takes over from Obiang. Until now it appears that his regime has served the interests of the multinational oil corporations. The failure of the US and Britain to give Equatorial Guinea warning of the attempted coup begs the questions as to whether the imperialists are now looking for an alternative to replace.'

Also in 2006 there were rumours that Obiang's son, 35-year-old Teodorin, was being groomed to succeed his father who has prostrate cancer and heart problems. It was said that Obiang's weight had dropped to around seven stone and that he wanted to leave office 'to fight against death'. Teodorin, equally as corrupt as his father – and his favourite son – was reinstated as Minister of Forestry when Obiang sacked his fifty-man cabinet in August 2006. Many said Teodorin was more like a 'minister for cutting down trees' after devastating hardwood forests largely to the benefit of his logging company. Teodorin, like the rest of the Obiang clan, enjoyed spending his country's money and that same month it was reported that with homes in Los Angeles, Buenos Aires and Paris, he paid a visit to South Africa and in just one weekend spent almost £1.1m on two Bentleys and a Lamborghini – as well as two luxury houses worth £3.7m. Both houses were renovated with a £100,000 home theatre audio system, a £40,000 air-conditioning system, a £3,500 fridge-freezer and a £1,000 ice-maker. At one point, George Ehlers, a South African builder who claimed that he was owed nearly £5m for work carried out for the Equatoguinean government, tried to seize the houses – an action strongly contested by Teodorin and his father, who said they were bought privately.

Teodorin once had a relationship with rap singer Eve on whom he spent a good deal of money but she reportedly left him after claims his father was a cannibal. Whether Teodorin will indeed take over from his father is still very much up in the air. Other members of the Obiang family and the major oil companies, are believed to favour Teodorin's younger brother Gabriel.

There is, of course, no freedom of speech in Equatorial Guinea. Those who dare to criticise the government are dealt with severely. (One French economist bent on exposing corruption in the country had the veins in his neck sliced open.) One political opponent, Pedro Moto, had his liver removed in 1993 and there was widespread speculation that Obiang then ate it.

And there is no such thing as a free press. Journalists are subject to harassment (in 2005 the editor of the Spanish-language service of the pan-African news agency AFROL received a phone call from presidential spokesman Miguel Ovono who accused him of 'waging a campaign against Equatorial Guinea' and warned him of the 'consequences' of what he reported). The government authorizes censorship of all publications and it has been known for the Ministry of Information to ask for copy to be submitted for approval before it is published. In June 2005, airport police in Bata seized 200 copies of *La Verdad*, a small CPDS newspaper and the country's only opposition publication, which were destined for distribution on the mainland. Equatorial Guinea once had three 'general interest' publications – all published rather sporadically; *La Gaceta* a Malabo-based monthly magazine printed in Spain and published by an employee of the Ministry of Information, Tourism and Culture, *El Correo Guineo Ecuatoriano*, a bi-monthly newspaper that was discontinued by the Gaceta group, and *Ebano*, a publication of the Ministry of Information which appeared perhaps twice a month. (Foreign celebrity and sports publications are on sale at foreign-owned grocery stores, but no newspapers and there are no book stores or news stands in the country.)

The government also dominates local radio broadcasting, owning Radio Malabo, officially known as National Radio of Equatorial Guinea. A private radio station, Radio Asonga, had the president's son as its proud owner.

Noted the 2006 human rights report: 'The government generally withheld access to domestic broadcasting from opposition parties and rarely referred to the opposition in anything but negative terms when broadcasting the news.

It is little wonder that there are repeated attempts to change the way things are run in Equatorial Guinea – even in the knowledge that reprisals will be brutal or fatal.

It is, of course, impossible to know what lies in store for the people of Equatorial Guinea. But Anthony Goldman, Africa analyst for Clearwater Research Services, said that the sudden arrival of oil wealth in what until a few years ago was one of the poorest countries in the world has 'created an explosive mix' in the country. 'It's had an unfortunate passage of dictatorships from the colonial period and then after independence – regimes of unparalleled brutality even in Africa. In the 1970s a third of the population were killed or fled into exile under the regime of Masias Nguema. His nephew seized power in 1979, promising to liberalise the country. And although now in theory it's a multi-party democracy, opposition supporters, diplomats and a number of human rights activists maintain that it remains a dictatorial regime, fuelled now by the arrival of oil.'

It is said that America does not want to criticise a country with valuable oil assets. In 2006, Secretary of State, Condoleezza Rice, hailed Obiang as a 'good friend' despite repeated criticism of his human rights and civil liberties record by her own department. Latterly, President Barack Obama posed for an official photograph with Obiang at a New York reception. The advocacy group Global Witness has been lobbying the United States to act against Obiang's

126

son Teodorin, a government minister. It says there is credible evidence that he spent millions buying a Malibu mansion and private jet using corruptly acquired funds – grounds for denying him a visa. Commented one political observer: 'it is still possible that the US government wishes to remove its "good friend" Obiang who is known to be in ill health. He has a number of sons who are all vying to succeed him. Obiang himself came to power by murdering his uncle. A messy power struggle amongst his family would draw in neighbouring Cameroon and Gabon to support rival factions. Not only would that pose a threat to the US control of the country's oil reserves, but it would potentially inflame the rest of West Africa.'

In March 2008, Obiang dissolved his parliament, announcing that municipal and legislative elections would be held on 4 May, and that a presidential vote was scheduled for 2010. In July 2008, the entire government of Prime Minister Ricardo Mangue Obama Nfuebea (a Bubi) resigned following Obiang's accusations of corruption and mismanagement. Nfuebea apolgised for 'not having been able to comply with all the wishes of his Excellency the President when it comes to achieving a developed and prosperous country.' Nfu Obiang named Ignacio Milam Tang as his new prime minister. Tang is a member of the Fang group and has enjoyed a good career under Obiang's rule. He was Minister of Justice and Worship from 1996 to 1998, then Minister of Youth and Sports from 1998 to 1999. In 1999 he was elected as the Second Vice-President of the Chamber of People's Representatives, and remained in that post until being appointed as Deputy Prime Minister for the Civil Service and Administrative Co-ordination in the government of Prime Minister Cándido Muatetema Rivas on 26 February 2001. After two years as Deputy Prime Minister he was appointed as Minister of State and Secretary-General of the Presidency on 11 February 2003. On 10 January 2006 it was announced that he had been appointed as Equatorial Guinea's Ambassador to Spain. He served in that position until being made Obiang's new prime minster.

Obiang appointed the new government headed by Tang on 14 July. A press release announced: 'In response to the circumstances surrounding His Excellency Ignacio Milam Tang, I hereby appoint him Prime Minister and head of government, with political and legal effect from today.' About half of the members of the previous government were brought back for Tang's government despite

Obiang describing them as 'one of the worst governments ever formed' and adding that the team 'has not done their work as they should have'. Commented *Afrol News*: 'Real powers in Equatorial Guinea are totally pinned in the Malabo presidency, which in practical terms fully controls budgets, day-to-day politics and law-making. President Obiang nevertheless has tried to distance himself increasingly from governments in an attempt to place responsibility for failures with the Prime Minister.' Tang was re-elected prime minister following Obiang's last election victory.

On 17 February 2009, it was reported that security forces in Equatorial Guinea had repelled an attack on the presidential palace. It said that the unidentified attackers were believed to have arrived on Bioko island by boat and were involved in a gun battle with guards at the palace for up to three hours. The shooting started around 3am and by daylight roadblocks had been set up. Obiang was said not to have been in residence at the time. One gunman was killed and a number of others were reported to have drowned when their boat was sunk by the country's navy. It was also reported that government helicopters and jets were deployed during the attack. Armoured vehicles blocked the entrance to the city's main hospital and only medical personnel were being allowed access. Police and soldiers had also taken up positions around the Clinic Guadeloupe, one of the country's main private clinics, in the city centre. State radio and television broadcasts continued as normal, but banks and public offices, as well as shops, were closed. Officials denied there had been an attempted coup, blaming 'rebel terrorists' from the Movement for the Emancipation of the Niger River Delta (MEND) an organisation which denied any involvement. MEND has fought for the 'fairer distribution of wealth from foreign oil' and normally confines its operations to southern Nigeria and its offshore oil installations. Equatorial Guinea said MEND had been involved in two Equatorial Guinea bank robberies in December 2007. But said Equatorial Guinean ambassador to London Augustin Nze Nfumu: 'I will categorically say there hasn't been any coup attempt in Equatorial Guinea at all ... it was a criminal act.'

Officials later accused Faustino Ondo Ebang, former leader of the opposition Popular Union Party and living in exile in Spain since 2007, of being behind the attempted coup.

Two days later, seventeen men were arrested in connection with the incident.

Amnesty International reported that nine of these were members of the opposition Popular Union Party who were detained without charge or trial. It said that at least two of those detained had been tortured in order to extract a confession. The nine were arrested without warrants between 18 February and 1 March 2009 in Bata, the main city on the mainland, and in Malabo. Two other men were arrested in Malabo on 22 March. Amnesty International said that the prisoners were interrogated by the police and accused of making telephone calls to Faustino Ondo Ebang in Spain. The AI report stated: 'Their arrest and detention violates Equatorial Guinean law which requires a warrant to carry out an arrest and stipulates that detainees must be informed of the charges against them and brought before a judge within 72 hours to legalize their detention. Amnesty International is concerned that Marcelino Nguema was tortured on 19 March and that Santiago Asumu was tortured while in detention in Bata central police station and on at least two other occasions since his transfer to Malabo. He is now in poor health as a result of the torture. Santiago Asumu had his hands and feet tied together and then suspended from a height and beaten all over the body. On one occasion in Malabo, the police tied his hands at the back and put him in a sack and then beat him. His mouth was stuffed with paper, presumably to stop him from screaming. At the same time he was asked for the names of soldiers who, the police claimed, would have taken part in the attack on the presidential palace with Faustino Ondó Ebang. The police further alleged that Faustino Ondó had sent Santiago Asumu to facilitate the attack, which he denied. As far as Amnesty International is aware, the other detainees have not been tortured or ill-treated. However, they are being held in overcrowded cells that lack sanitation and hygienic facilities, which amounts to inhuman and cruel treatment.' In May 2009 a French judge announced he was launching an investigation into claims by 'corruption watchdog' Transparency International France that Obiang and two other African leaders acquired millions of dollars' worth or property in Paris and on the French Riviera, as well as luxury cars, all bought with embezzled public money. The allegations were denied but became known as the case of 'ill-gotten gains'. A French appeal court dismissed the case saying that no action could be taken against foreign heads of state. European newspapers have reported that Obiang and his family frequently embark on frenzied shopping sprees at the exclusive quarter of Faubourg Saint Honore in Paris. The family also owns property in America. Obiang has two homes in suburban Washington, DC, one valued at $2m and the other at $1.3m, according to *The Washington Post*. Obiang's son Teodorin who attended Pepperdine University in Malibu, California, maintains a $6.9m mansion in Los Angeles. Teodorin drives around Paris in a Rolls Royce or Lamborghini and once made an $11m offer on a New York condo owned by Adnan Khashoggi but was rejected by the building's board, according to *The Nation* magazine. An editor of an energy newsletter called Obiang's son 'the closest thing there is to African oil'. It is estimated that as much as $7m have been deposited at an American bank (some of it directly by American oil companies) and then transferred to secret offshore accounts.

In July 2009, a 107-page report 'Well Oiled: Oil and Human Rights in Equatorial Guinea' said that the country's government had set new low standards of political and economic 'malfeasance' in handling its billions of dollars in oil revenue instead of improving the lives of its citizens. Said Arvind Ganesan, director of the Business and Human Rights Program at Human Rights Watch: 'Since oil was discovered there in the early 1990s, Equatorial Guinea's gross domestic product (GDP) has increased more than 5,000 per cent, and the country has become the fourth-largest oil producer in sub-Saharan Africa. At the same time, living standards for the country's 500,000 people have not substantially improved. Here is a country where people should have the per capita wealth of Spain or Italy, but instead they live in conditions comparable to Chad or the Democratic Republic of the Congo. This is a testament to the government's corruption, mismanagement, and callousness toward its own people ... The government's failure to provide basic social services violates its obligations under the International Covenant on Economic, Social and Cultural Rights.'

In August 2009, much was made of the thirtieth anniversary of the coup that saw Obiang take over the presidency from his uncle. In the words of Obiang's government: 'In 1979, after the devastation of a decade under the tyrannical President Macias, then Lieutenant Colonel Obiang took control of the government and was named President of the Supreme Military Council.' In that same year 'a presidential decree made him vice-minister of the Popular Armed Forces.' The official line continued: 'Obiang became President of the Republic for an initial seven-year term. He was re-elected to additional terms in 1989, 1996 and 2003. President Obiang won re-election once again in 1996. Infrastructure and housing is now being rebuilt more quickly as new water, sewage and drainage are being installed and hundreds of miles of new roadways are being built to connect all of Equatorial Guinea's cities and towns. Healthcare and education also top the agenda as new, modern state-of-art hospitals and clinics are being built and staffed and teachers are being trained to better teach students.'

The election outcome could more or less be predicted. Obiang won 97.1 per cent of the votes in 2002 and took 98 and 99 seats respectively in 2004 and 2008 out of 100.

As human rights observers noted: 'Those elections were marred by serious irregularities. The 2008 campaign was considered freer than earlier ones. But there was a strong presence by military and security personnel on the streets of all major towns, limits on free-dom of movement, harassment of opposition supporters and voters, restrictions on access by international journalists, and numerous irregularities at polling places.'

In short, Obiang wins every election by a massive majority.

Patrick Smith, editor of *Africa Confidential* magazine, said that in latter times there has been a lot of unease within the Equatorial Guinean military, particularly over the succession issue. 'It is felt that President Obiang's health is not good, and that should he die precipitously, there would be a bloody struggle to succeed him. And one of the key characters likely to lead that struggle would be his son, Teodorin, who is heartily disliked by many other people in the Equatorial Guinea military.'

Justice Minister Ruben Mangue said that rumours of a power struggle are commonplace everywhere but – he insists – com-pletely untrue: 'The president has been elected for seven years. The president is healthy ... it is not serious to talk about the succession to the president now.'

Radical newspaper *Dissident Voice* which campaigns for political and social justice provided its own take on just how Equatorial Guinea is run:

131

The main difference between the deposed president and the current one is that Obiang knows how to read the signs of the times and to adapt himself accordingly. This has allowed him to hold on to power for thirty years, count on foreign support and enrich himself enormously thanks to the oil industry, also under his control.

The past thirty years can indeed be described as golden thirty years for Obiang, but not for the great majority of Equatorial Guinea's inhabitants. Country reports published by the World Bank, the European Union and some of the United Nations agencies, let alone those by non governmental organisations, especially those devoted to human rights and human development, present a quite different reality.

Obiang is willing to play the democratic game in front of the international community, because in each game he marks the cards and keeps the best while deals the rest.

If appearances have to be kept up of regular elections, of honouring international treaties, of adhering to foreign initiatives on transparency, accountability and good governance, for Obiang this is no problem. He lets the opposition win a parliamentary seat; he signs international treaties only to honour them in the breach, and varnishes his masterwork with glowing propaganda about the government's good works.

Obiang has many good friends who just happen to govern powerful countries. These convince public opinion that Obiang's scam is legitimate and only needs a few tweaks and minor improvements. To that end, they offer technical assistance and cooperation, while making clear there is no great urgency. Since oil production started in Equatorial Guinea in the mid 90s, his friends have become even more reliable than ever, despite knowing the reality all too well.

The 2004 Department of State report on Equatorial Guinea accurately summarised its political situation: 'Citizens did not have the ability to change their government peacefully.'

In 2009 the Department refers to the country as a 'nominally multi-party Republic with strong domination by the executive branch.'

For his part, Obiang thinks it wise to take preventive measures. He sends soldiers and policemen to assassinate, kidnap and torture his 'enemies', and in general to make life difficult for political opponents.

In spite of this and of the fact that there is no shortage of people willing to get their share of the enormous oil cake in exchange for loyalty, some still remain who do not give up. Some of these string along with Obiang's pretense of democracy. Others prefer to try and oust him.

Considering their actions so far, it can safely be said that Obiang has clearly defeated them all. He intimidates, persecutes and entertains members of the first group, according to his whims. He attacks members of the second whenever he can. These have managed to discomfit him once, but Obiang's friends and luck have been on his side.

Neither group of the opposition can claim that their respective strategies have come anywhere close to achieving their goals. The reverse is true, as chances of success seem to be inversely proportional to the increase in their actions.

Playing Obiang's democracy game is not an easy task. If a player does not perform as expected, other players will not take them seriously. Equatorial Guinea's leader of the parliamentary opposition declares again and again to the international community, to the media, to various international political institutions, that his party plays by Obiang's rules and also reassures the world that his party will only use non-violent means to achieve power.

But if the international community does not demand that Obiang play by internationally accepted rules to stay in power, why does the opposition think they have to do so? It seems the international community accepts opposition to Obiang as long as its leaders give up their people's right to resist the Obiang regime's human rights violations.

Philosophers dealt with the problem of using legitimate violence against an aggression many centuries ago. Since the 13th century it is accepted that 'in the case of a deadly attack, there is more obligation to protect one's own life than the attacker's.'

If a political party which opposes a never ending dictatorship renounces legitimate defence against its violence, it is delegitimizing itself, because it actually helps the dictatorship it claims to oppose. When this party seeks support from international actors, despite their party's poor record of resistance and even knowing full well their petition will be met with indifference, they are digging their own political grave.

It is true that a legitimate defence requires another condition, namely that there are reasonable chances of success. In this respect it has to be noted that it is all about not giving up the right to legitimate resistance. Further, there can be no likelihood of success if the possibility of resistance is totally abandoned.

The non-parliamentary opposition, made up of several small groups, has not renounced political violence. But its failure, too, is obvious and due mainly to lack of popular, militant support, to splits and internecine fighting and other shortcomings.

The option of a coup d'état has not yielded useful results. Nor is there much chance that it will. The lack of a popular militia and bad planning, along with the use of foreign mercenaries, explain the failure. Day after day, Obiang increases his own security, and he can count on foreign support. It seems that only a palace coup, like the one Obiang himself authored 30 years ago, is likely to succeed.

It can be said that the opposition too, like Obiang, have placed their hopes in foreign hands. The difference between the two camps is that European and North American Presidents and Prime Ministers prefer oil in their own countries to ensuring human rights in Equatorial Guinea.

Although he initially said an election would take place in 2010, Obiang announced on 16 October 2009 that the election would now be on 29 November and that campaigning would officially begin on 5 November. As Human Rights Watch noted: 'The tight timetable and the government's refusal to make the voter rolls public have severely limited the opposition's ability to campaign and win support. Voter registration was completed in October, but the electoral lists still had not been made public as of mid-November. The opposition voiced suspicion that this move was intended to keep opposition supporters off the rolls. The government claimed that it could not release the names because opposition supporters might use the information to harass other parties.

'The opposition is hampered by skewed coverage in the government-controlled media that heavily favors the ruling party and by the virtual absence of a free press. Similarly, although the government has provided financing for all parties, the ruling party had far greater access to state funds and other resources than did the opposition.

'Opposition parties also complained of harassment and intimidation as they carried out campaign activities in various parts of the country. Although Human Rights Watch was not in a position to confirm directly their allegations of attacks and other abuses during campaigning in October and November, the Obiang government and ruling party have a long history of cracking down on opposition activities in election years, often citing "security reasons" in the wake of real or perceived coup attempts.'

Human Rights Watch noted on 25 November 2009: 'No independent and impartial body exists in Equatorial Guinea to oversee the electoral process or consider election-related complaints, raising additional serious doubts about conditions for a genuinely free and fair vote. The National Election Commission is controlled by the ruling party and headed by Obiang's minister of the interior, a prominent member of his party.

'The conditions imposed by the government of Equatorial Guinea on international election observers do not permit them to carry out independent foreign monitoring. The terms and scope of the foreign observation missions were made public in an October presidential order. It interferes with the independence and freedom of movement of foreign election monitors in several ways:

- Observers will be permitted to travel to witness the vote only 'in accordance with the program established for that purpose by the government' (articles 11, 12, and 18).
- They are to report any 'problems' or 'anomalies' directly to the government (arts. 20 and 22).
- Their ability to speak to the 'official news media' about their 'activities' during voting is subject to approval by the Interior Ministry (art. 21).
- They may issue their findings publicly after the voting has concluded, but the content of their statements must be

coordinated with the National Electoral Commission, which is controlled by the ruling party (arts. 24 and 25).

- They are prohibited from 'interfering' in any 'political matters' or making 'controversial statements' about the election authorities or 'disparaging' remarks about the government, the political parties, or candidates (arts. 4, 22, and 23).

'These conditions are inconsistent with the Declaration of Principles of International Election Observation and Code of Conduct for International Election Observers, as endorsed by intergovernmental and nongovernmental organizations conducting election observation, including the African Union.'

Obiang again took 97 per cent of the votes amidst claims of corruption from his election rivals. Commented Arvind Ganesan, director of the Business and Human Rights Program at Human Rights Watch: 'President Obiang claims that he's committed to the rule of law. But his actions time and again are those of a dictator determined to hang onto power and control of the country's oil money.'

On 14 January 2010 *New Zimbabwe* reported that continental hospitality and leisure group African Sun had shelved plans to venture into Equatorial Guinea due to the country's political instability. Speaking at an analyst presentation for the company's full year results, Group Chief executive officer, Shingi Munyeza said African Sun had decided to take a cautious approach to its investment in the oil rich nation, stating: 'With regards to Equatorial Guinea we have decided to take a cautious approach, the hotels are there but closed at the moment due to the political situation in that country.' African Sun was embroiled in a legal battle with a group of local architects in Equatorial Guinea over non payment of $16m for construction work done on a hotel property the group was meant to run under a management contract agreement.

In February, commentator Eric Leech summed up the state of Equatorial Guinea: 'Asphalt parking lots cradling the slew of SUV's parked haphazardly in front of the air-conditioned office buildings where oil business is done. Beyond these fancy buildings, makeshift homes are built among dirty, smile-less faces. Its not that there isn't signs of money being spent here, just not where it is needed (education, water, electricity, healthcare, etc.). The executives are told to keep their mouth shut or they will find themselves on the first plane back to America. Those who criticize Obiang's regime end up in jail, or much worse!'

In April 2010, an Equatorial Guinea court sentenced seven Nigerians to twelve years in prison on terrorism charges for their role in the February 2009 attack on the presidential palace – the attack officials denied at the time was an attempted coup. Two of the men were later reported to have died in detention. It was reported that the Nigerian embassy was not granted access to the prisoners, was not officially informed of their arrests, the charges against them or the 'status of proceedings and the death of two of them.' The court also released four Equatorial Guineans, all members of the opposition People's Union Party. Seven had been released in March through a lack of evidence.

On 25 July 2010, under the headline 'Now "cannibal" dictator who set Simon Mann free bids to join Commonwealth', Sharon Church for *The Mail on Sunday* reported that Obiang was seeking admission to the Commonwealth. She wrote: 'Equatorial Guinea's president, Teodoro Obiang, will submit evidence of his "civilised" treatment of the mercenary to the organisation in an attempt to prove that his state meets its membership criteria, which includes respect for human rights.' A source was quoted as saying that 'Obiang has already started to use various well-connected friends of his regime in New York, Washington and London to get out word to representatives of key Commonwealth nations that Simon Mann's release demonstrates he really is very civilised. The serious subtext to this is that he believes he has been misrepresented and that he has not been given credit for how much he has been trying to improve the lives of his people. He wants Equatorial Guinea to have a seat at the table with other African nations that are Commonwealth members. He thinks that is his due and he believes that, from the point of view of Britain, it is a rather practical idea. Equatorial Guinea could help shift the balance in terms of dependency on Saudi oil.'

In August 2010, Equatorial Guinea defended the execution of four former government officials convicted of attempting to assassinate Obiang during the attack on the presidential palace in February 2009. The four – José Abeso Nsue, a former captain of the country's land forces, his deputy Manuel Ndong Anseme, member of the presidential security team Alipio Ndong Asumu and former customs chief Jacinto Michá Obiang – were executed immediately after being convicted by a military court in Malabo of being 'criminally responsible and the authors of an attack on the head of state and representative of the government, terrorism and treason.' The executions focussed the world's eyes once again on Equatorial Guinea. A few days before they took place, a working group from the Independent United Nations group visited the country to investigate activities of mercenaries in the country and their impact on human rights. Chairman Amada Benavides de Pérez and colleague José-Luis Gomez del Prado said they strongly condemned the executions noting that they followed a 'summary trial that severely lacked due process ... this points to severe shortcomings in the implementation of international human rights standards in the administration of justice by the Government of Equatorial Guinea.'

The two also condemned the decision to execute on the same day of conviction, leaving the accused no time to appeal. 'The [working] group could not obtain information on how the four men, who had taken refuge in Benin, were brought back into the country. They appear not to have been subjected to formal extradition procedures.'

The group focussed on the attempted coups both in 2009 and in 2004. Concerning Mann's 2004 coup, the group reported: 'The working group considers that this is a clear example of the link between the phenomenon of mercenaries and private military and security companies as a means of violating the sovereignty of the State. In this case, the mercenaries involved were mostly former personnel of private military and security companies and some were still employed by a private military and security companies as the case of two employees of the company Meteoric Tactical Systems providing security to diplomats of Western Embassies in Baghdad – among which to the Ambassador of Switzerland.

'The group received information regarding the 2004 and 2008 trials of those arrested in connection with this coup attempt, including the British citizen Simon Mann and the South African Nick du Toit. The group notes that all foreigners linked to this coup attempt were pardoned in November 2009 by the President. Nonetheless, a number of reports indicated that trials failed to comply with international human rights standards and that some of the accused had been subjected to torture and ill-treatment.'

Mrs Pérez and Mr Gomez del Prado issued a series of preliminary recommendations to authorities in Equatorial Guinea, including 'full information in a transparent manner regarding all matters connected to the armed attack by alleged mercenaries on 17 February 2009.' During their five-day visit to the country, Mrs Pérez and Mr Gomez del Prado held meetings with Obiang and numerous senior officials of the executive, judiciary and legislative as well as with representatives of the UN, political parties, diplomatic corps and civil service. The two experts made some 'preliminary recommendations, to the Equatorial Guinea authorities saying the working group:

Requests the authorities of Equatorial Guinea to provide full information in a transparent manner regarding the 17 February 2009 incident, and in particular, that: all judgements rendered in the criminal cases related to the attack be made available to the public, in accordance with article 14(1) of the International Covenant on Civil and Political Rights that the State of Equatorial Guinea has ratified;

That explanations be given as to how the four ex militaries refugees in Benin – José Abeso Nsue, Manuel Ndong Anseme, Alipio Ndong Asumu and Jacinto Michá Obiang – were brought back to Equatorial Guinea to face a military trial and on the due process guarantees they were given in conformity with international human rights instruments; information regarding their summary execution immediately after being sentenced, without a possibility to appeal the decision;

Calls upon the Government, in accordance with articles 36 and 37 of the 1963 Vienna Convention on Consular Relations, if this has not yet been done, to grant the Nigerian Embassy access without delay to the five Nigerians currently in detention and to inform it without delay of any case of death of its nationals. The Government should also grant the ICRC access to the detainees;

Requests the Government to reply to its communication of 2006 related to allegations of torture and ill-treatment related to the mercenaries tried in relation to the 2004 failed coup.

Invites the State of Equatorial Guinea to accede to the 1989 International Convention against the recruitment, use, financing and training of mercenaries as a matter of priority; encourages the Government to consider developing national legislation to criminalize

139

the presence of mercenaries and mercenary-related acts and to regulate the activities of private military and security companies and their employees.

Encourages the Government to carefully consider the proposals of the working group for a possible new legal instrument regulating private military and security companies and to support the establishment of an open-ended working group with the task of developing a new Convention on this matter.

The report added that the working group was fully aware of how Equatorial Guinea had experienced several coup attempts, and added: 'In this regard the working group believes that in addition to the right and the duty of states to defend its borders and natural resources, the Government would reduce its vulnerability to mercenary attacks, by promoting and strengthening democracy, economical, social and cultural rights and development in general as well as good governance. Therefore, the group calls on the Government to ensure free political participation, the independence of the judiciary and a transparent and efficient administration of justice.' The full report read:

The working group is grateful to the Equatorial Guinean Government for its invitation. The Group held meetings in Malabo with the Head of State, Teodoro Obiang Nguema Mbasogo, and senior officials of the executive, the judiciary and the legislature, including the Third Deputy Prime Minister for Human Rights, the Presidential Advisor on Human Rights, the Minister and Vice-Minister of Justice, the Deputy Defence Minister and the Deputy Minister of Foreign Affairs, the Attorney General, the President of the Supreme Court of Justice, the Speaker of Parliament as well as the Vice President of the National Human Rights Commission. The independent experts also met with representatives of political parties and civil society, and held meeting with the United States Ambassador as well as representatives from theworking group:Embassy of Spain, France, Nigeria and South Africa. It met with the UN Resident Coordinator as well as with representatives of a private military and security company operating in Equatorial Guinea.

140

The experts also visited Punta Europa, the port facility of oil companies on the island of Bioko, to get information on the security arrangements of oil companies in this area.

Concerning the 17 February 2009 attack on the presidential palace by alleged mercenaries, the working group received information that the Government arrested seven Nigerians and nine equato-Guineans in relation to this attack. The working group regrets the lack of transparency on the part of the authorities, in particular that it did not have access to the judicial decisions, nor to those who stood trial and are still in detention.

The group is particularly concerned at the information that on 21 August 2010, three former military officers and one civilian were executed after a summary military trial in which they were found guilty on treason and terrorism charges. The working group strongly condemns this execution, which follows a summary trial that severely lacked due process and the fact that the sentence was carried out the same day denying the defendants all possibility of appeal. The group could not obtain information on how the four men, who had taken refuge in Benin, were brought back into the country. They appear not to have been subjected to formal extradition procedures.

Two other civilians were sentenced in the same military trial to 20 years imprisonment. The working group is concerned that the guaranties to due process were not respected in this case, in particular that these civilians were tried by a military court after having been acquitted on 5 April 2010 by a civilian court in a first instance.

The working group has received information that among the seven Nigerians arrested, two have died in detention while the five others have been sentenced to 12 years' imprisonment. It has also received information that the Nigerian Embassy has not been granted access to them, nor officially been informed of their arrests, the charges held against them, the status of proceedings and the death of two of them. Several sources also raised doubts regarding their involvement in the attack and the lack of evidence presented at the trial.

The lack of transparency regarding these trials, despite the repeated requests by the working group to access judicial decisions as well as visit the detainees, points to severe shortcomings in the implementation of international human rights standards in the administration of justice by the Government of Equatorial Guinea.

141

Amnesty International also condemned the executions claiming that the men were detained in Black Beach prison where they were tortured into giving false confessions. Criticising the government's legal system, Amnesty's African director, Erwin van der Borght, stated: 'These men were convicted after an unfair trial, sentenced to death and executed with chilling speed without having the slightest opportunity to appeal their sentence. Equatorial Guinea must put an end to the abductions, torture and executions it currently carries out under the pretense of justice.' The Equatorial Guinean government said the men had received a fair and open trial and had been provided with legal advisors. But Amnesty International, too, said the men were living in exile in Benin at the time of the alleged coup attempt. Said an AI spokesmen: 'They were convicted of attacking the presidential palace when they had gone into exile much earlier and for other reasons, because they were being persecuted already, so their exile was not connected to the attack last year.'

Two other officers were jailed for twenty years for their involvement in the attack.

But with the eyes of the world now regularly alighting upon Equatorial Guinea, some changes seem to be taking place. But one cannot help but be cynical. The derelict capital Malabo is being transformed with new housing, office and shop developments; albeit next to the shanty towns. The installation of an Italian marble fountain outside the Spanish gothic cathedral in the main square might look impressive but less than half of the country's population has access to good drinking water. The running water distribution network of Malabo is described as 'obsolete' while that in Bata is 'almost inexistent'. The water supply for the rest of the population is provided through shallow wells, non-protected sources, or rivers. The sanitation infrastructures are described as 'insufficient' and not complying with 'current standards'.

The construction of a new Malabo is being undertaken by Obiang's new best friend – China. The country was quick to take advantage of Obiang's fall out with America following the Riggs bank scandal after which he withdrew all his money from the bank. China won drilling rights and a Chinese work force was taken on to help with re-building – paid for by China.

In September 2010, it was reported that Filiberto Ntutumu, Equatorial Guinea's Minister of Education, Science and Sport had met with teachers and 'education professionals' to discuss future plans for improving the country's education system. Ntutumu said that two themes of the meetings – 'Thinking about general education' and 'Planning, education management and legal tools to regulate the functioning of education' – stressed how important education was. The guidelines for the new rules included:

In order to maintain school safety and encourage learning:

- *Let peace reign in all schools, including the directors, teachers and students and avoid any conflict.*
- *Prohibit all sharp material such as scissors, razors, etc. and impose expulsion of one week for violation.*
- *Fights between peers require a one month suspension.*

With regard to discipline:

- *The director must remain in their assigned location daily.*
- *Attendance and punctuality, both for the directors, teachers, and for the students, is required.*
- *Any dispute between students and teachers can lead to expulsion.*

For a quality of education and training it is recommended:

- *Conduct training seminars.*
- *Teachers must present the agenda for their classes at the beginning of the course.*
- *Objective assessment of students.*
- *Cleanliness and order in schools.*
- *All students must wear uniforms.*
- *Prohibit all vices and unhealthy behaviors such as counterfeiting grades, sexual harassment, alcoholism, smoking, prostitution among students, etc.*

World Habitat Day – held on the first Monday of October every year – in 2010 again brought focus on Equatorial Guinea when Amnesty International called for an end to forced evictions in the country. Around 1,000 families since 2003 have been forcibly evicted from their homes to make room for roads, up-market housing, hotels and shopping centres. Homes have been demolished in Malabo, Bata and other large towns. Many of the houses demolished, reported AI 'were solid structures in well-established neighbourhoods and the vast majority of the occupants had title to the land.' The report added: 'Despite promises of relocation for some of the victims, to date no one has been re-housed or compensated. Even the houses promised to the victims will have to be bought at a cost that far exceeds their ability to pay, and the houses are located far from the city and from their work and schools. Thousands more are at risk as the authorities embark on a program of urban regeneration. The new wealth brought about by the discovery of oil in the mid-1990s has led to pressure on the land for commercial purposes, as well as up-market housing. In addition, the authorities have started to rehabilitate the main cities and their infrastructure. On several occasions, the media has reported the publicly-expressed intentions of the authorities to rid the cities of the chambolismo (shanty towns). Under these initiatives, many more families risk being forcibly evicted from their homes.'

Chapter 11

Freedom

On 2 November 2009, Mann was given a complete pardon by Equatorial president Obiang on 'humanitarian grounds', believed to be because of Mann's ailing health – he had had a hernia operation earlier that year. He had served fifteen months of the 34-year sentence. The pardon was officially given as Mann, dressed in a white shirt and blue tie, sat on a wooden bench in a room at Black Beach prison. Speaking after the pardon ceremony Mann said: 'I have felt like a guest here and not like a prisoner. I have been well treated throughout. I was able to do exercise every morning in my cell, which is why I look fit. The worst thing has been to be away from my wife and children.' Observed one witness: 'He was very emotional. There were diplomats waiting for him and speeches were made.'

Channel 4 News correspondent Sue Turton was at the scene to report on Mann's last days in Equatorial Guinea. 'Simon Mann's brother and sister were told last Friday that the pardon was imminent and they flew out on a charter plane over the weekend. They went to the prison and collected him and then they all went across to one of the leading hotels there.

'When he was sentenced one of the things the judge did say was that as well as being incarcerated for thirty-four years he was also banned for returning to Equatorial Guinea for decades and decades – which promoted quite a rife smile on his face at the time. So it is expected that he will actually get on that charter plane and it will take him back home again.

'There have been rumours that this was going to happen for just over a month now due to worries about his sickness – he's had two hernia operations in prison since he was sentenced. For President Obiang they don't want his health to have deteriorated any further before he gets to go home.

'So I think in many ways it is compassionate grounds. It is Obiang's last roll of the dice – the last chance he gets to use Simon Mann to show he is this benevolent leader and he's done the right thing by releasing him.'

Mann was released along with four others of the convicted plotters who were given 24 hours to leave the country. A statement said: 'After his release, the offender is obliged to leave the country in the non-extendible period of 24 hours and are [sic] strictly prohibited from returning to the Republic of Equatorial Guinea.' Said Communications Minister Jeronimo Osa Osa Ekoro: 'The amnesty is total. They are free. They have already left prison and they have 24 hours to leave Guinea for the destination of their choice.'

Miguel Mifuno, an adviser to the Equatorial Guinea government, said Mann was pardoned because he had been 'sufficiently punished and has co-operated well. In particular, he gave a number of statements to Scotland Yard detectives while in Black Beach prison. Simon Mann conducted himself in exemplary fashion during his trial and his incarceration in Equatorial Guinea. He has some health problems and he was operated. He is now in good health but the president thinks he should now be allowed to live in peace with his family.'

But this would still not have been reassurance from a president notorious for barbaric treatment of anyone who opposed him. Severo Moto had told Mann that if he ever returned to Equatorial Guinea while Obiang was still in power, he would be tortured and murdered and Obiang would eat his testicles. He was also reported to have pledged to sodomise Mann before skinning him alive and parading his body through Malabo.

In *The Independent* on 4 November 2009, under the headline 'Bungled Coup: Lines of inquiry' reporter Cahal Milmo asked the following questions:

- Will Simon Mann stand by his testimony to a court in Equatorial Guinea that Mark Thatcher was part of the 'management team' for the coup?

- Will the mercenary also continue to insist that Mr X, the billionaire, was 'the Cardinal' – the powerful businessman who originated the coup plot?
- Did the CIA blow the whistle on the coup attempt to protect the interests of American oil companies?
- Did the Spanish authorities give tacit approval to the plan to replace President Obiang with Severo Moto, an opposition leader in exile in Madrid?
- What knowledge did Britain have of the plans for the coup and did London seek to warn the Obiang regime of what was happening?

It is believed that Mann's co-operation in naming accomplices helped secure a release, timed to coincide with a visit to the country by South African president Jacob Zuma. Further, it was timed three weeks ahead of presidential elections – something of a surprise in a country where compassion – no matter what the timing – is so alien. Claims that Mann had posed a security risk were denied. Retorted Equatorial Guinea's ambassador Nze Nfumu: 'Tell these people that they are writing novels; if they want to make another movie on that let them invent stories. The man has been there almost two years. I don't know what security risk. I can't commend such nonsense.' Nick du Toit and three South African mercenaries were pardoned at the same time.

But it is still felt that Equatorial Guinea will still fester over the attempted coup. Said one of Mann's former colleagues: 'One should not underestimate the extent to which the EG government wants this to be the start of a process that gets to the truth about this operation. They want an "in" with the world community, but not at the expense of getting at those who tried to undermine them. Simon was genuinely freed on compassionate grounds, but he co-operated with the EG authorities and told them just who was responsible for the whole operation.'

Also involved in Mann's release was former Conservative MP Rupert Allason, a military and intelligence expert who had started up a correspondence with Nfumu in the summer of 2008 and met up with him in August that year. Allason said he had become involved at the request of a 'mutual friend' of Mann's. Working with Greg Wales, Allason's latter negotiations had taken five weeks. When

Mann's release was finally announced, Allason commented: 'it has been a rather intense last five weeks. I thought he would be released on 10 or 12 October but there were complications ... I rang Sarah on the Thursday. She was vaguely aware of my existence and vaguely aware I'd been active on behalf of Simon. When I asked her to come up to London, she was very sceptical, not surprisingly because I think the Manns have been the victims of every kind of scam over the last six years. I told her I would get the ambassador to give her a call within the next ten minutes and that persuaded her we were in business.'

Allason added: 'The ambassador has behaved with a great deal of generosity and personal trust.' He had nothing but praise for Greg Wales, the man members of the coup felt has escaped justice, but who had actually been instrumental in their release. 'Greg Wales became aware that I was trying to help. Everything he has done in the last five weeks that I am aware of has been solely about obtaining Simon's release. He has not put a foot wrong.' Of the others connected with the coup, Allason said: 'I have no idea what is going to happen to Thatcher. I have never met this businessman, don't know anything about him. I have no idea what is going to happen to Archer. I think his books are garbage.'

Mann's brother Edward and sister Sarah Grootenhuis hired a private plane, reportedly at a cost of £100,000 to travel out and return with him. A family statement said: 'Everyone is profoundly grateful to the president and the government of Equatorial Guinea. The whole family is overjoyed at the prospect of finally welcoming Simon home after five-and-a-half long years away.'

Mann finally stepped on to British soil at Luton Airport at 1.43pm on 4 November 2009. In a statement read out by a family representative, he said: 'This is the most wonderful homecoming I could ever imagine. There hasn't been a moment during the last five and half years when I have not dreamt of one day being back in Britain. I am hugely grateful to President Obiang for releasing me. It's the best early Christmas present my family and I could ever have imagined.'

The flight home had been an emotional one with a source reporting: 'The pilot of the plane approached Simon and told him he was seven hours' flying time from London. Simon simply shook his hand and told him, "That's music to my ears." He was very emotional. And when he finally stepped on to the tarmac at Luton he had to wipe away a tear of elation ... He spent much of his flight home talking about son Arthur. He was absolutely fizzing with excitement. He couldn't stop talking about seeing Arthur for the first time.'

As the BBC's security correspondent Frank Gardner said: 'He's going to see a son he's never seen, who was born when he was in prison. This is a man, who if he had served his whole sentence, would have come out in his 90s.'

Mann's cousin, Lady Celia Norris, was just one family member relieved to see him home. She said: 'It's amazing that he's been released. It's wonderful news and a huge relief for us all. The most fantastic thing is he will be seeing his son for the first time. It's going to be a very emotional time for them both. The family has really suffered since he's been locked up. When I first heard the news, it was horrible. We all asked why did he have to do it. It was incredibly stupid of him; it's a ridiculous situation for him to get into as a married man with children. As an ex-member of the SAS, he has always lived a life of excitement, but this was going too far. It's remarkable they let him out. He was guilty but he did not deserve the sentence he was given. Thank God he is home.'

After arriving at Luton, Mann headed to London's King Edward VII hospital for medical checks.

The news of Mann's release prompted a response from those who had been involved in the attempted coup – including Severo Moto, the man who had hoped to take over the rule of Equatorial Guinea. Moto said: 'I am very, very pleased for the man who wanted to help me. Obiang is also happy because he got Mann to say what he wanted him to.'

Mark Thatcher said he was 'absolutely delighted that Simon will be reunited with his family at last,' and Greg Wales – who had always strenuously denied any involvement in the plot – added that he was 'very happy at last that my good friends in Equatorial Guinea have treated my good friend Simon Mann with such humanity.'

Mann's release also sparked 'debate' on the internet. Some were pleased he had returned safely, reunited with the four-year-old son he had never seen. Others simply felt he had got what he deserved:

Wishing you the speediest of returns back to the UK Simon, I hope you are swiftly re-united with your wife and your son, who you have never seen, and a fantastic first evening with friends and family. Then I hope you wake up in the middle of the night, stumble blindly unfamiliar with your surroundings not being a prison cell, stub your toe, get an infectious blood disease from it and die! Mercenary Simon Mann flies in from Equatorial Guinea, his five-year jail ordeal over. Aww diddums. Did the nasty men treat you all horrible, just 'cause you tried to pick up guns in Harare to go onto violently overthrow another country? Honestly, these Africans have no respect for ex-Etonians. I'd lie my way out of things and implicate everyone you can, make yourself look like a helpless pawn in someone else's game. Look forward to reading the book at Christmas, hopefully the royalties will be donated to a worthy cause.

Good heavens ... are you trying to be witty? There must be some excuse, I suppose, for your seemingly deliberate attempt to ignore what everyone else recognises. Simon Mann (an old-Etonian, incidentally, not 'ex-') was granted the Queen's commission and served this country in a British regiment. He set out to remove from power a dictator whose reputation, in a continent where dictators set high standards of awfulness, is unequalled even by his Zimbabwean friend. The Intelligence services of both the UK and the US knew exactly what was planned and their democratic masters approved. Who would not? You write that you hope he will die and you style him 'Mercenary'. Mercenaries have an honoured place in history ...

Both Mann and du Toit were bitter and angry at a decision by British police chiefs that there was insufficient evidence to pursue Mark Thatcher or the wealthy businessman (who had hired Margaret Thatcher's PR guru Lord Bell to rebut the allegations against him, which he said were an elaborate set-up). They were also not happy that Greg Wales had escaped retribution. Wales, in turn, said he had voluntarily approached police investigators in Britain when he was concerned crucial pieces of evidence were missing from their inquiry. (The role of Scotland Yard was to ascertain whether any aspect of the attempted coup took place on British soil and Mann was interviewed four times while in jail.) Wales also said he had been involved in negotiations for several weeks with Ambassador Augustin Nfumu in London to secure Mann's release. Wales admitted that money was initially part of the negotiation but that Nfumu had dropped the demand. Good public relations for Equatorial Guinea were more important. Wales said: 'I think you could say that the government there thought they had treated Simon very well and had dealt with him reasonably and it would have been very unfair if anything else was said.'

At the time of Mann's release, a Metropolitan Police spokesman said: 'We can confirm we are investigating whether any offences may have been disclosed in this country. We are aware of developments but are not prepared to discuss them further. We are liaising with the Crown Prosecution Service. Inquiries continue. The Counter Terrorism Command is investigating.'

Despite denials that any payment had helped secure Mann's release, it was strongly rumoured that £200,000 had been paid to the Obiang regime – a fee reduced from several millions after two months of negotiations. Nick du Toit said Mann had talked openly about paying off government ministers and told him: 'I'm getting out of here. But it's already cost me more than £400,000 and they still want more.' Du Toit added: 'I got the impression he had paid government ministers. He had got his people to transfer £315,000 to one of them and £250,000 to the other. Now, he was openly talking about it. There was no shame or secrecy. Of course, I knew corruption was not even a dirty word in some parts of Africa. This was bribery pure and simple.'

Du Toit was later to go further with his claims, describing how at one point, Mann sat next to the Attorney General of Equatorial Guinea at Black Beach prison with the two men discussing large sums of money. It was said that Mann even borrowed the Attorney General's mobile phone to call home – and then went on to berate his wife Amanda for fifty minutes for not providing the funds to buy his way out of prison. He apparently asked what was holding up the bank transfer and when would the money reach West Africa. Du Toit was one of the four fellow prisoners watching the scene who had been summoned to one of the occasional meetings with the Attorney General in a ground room at the prison. Du Toit said that Mann 'seemed so relaxed, almost unaware of us. Then he wanted to shake my hand and was only slightly embarrassed that I was shuffling over to him in chains. He asked how I was and I said I was fine. It was unreal.'

However, the suggestion of a 'bribe' was challenged by Adam Roberts, author of *The Wonga Coup* who stated in the *Guardian*: 'I don't think there has been a grand deal between Britain and

151

Equatorial Guinea to secure Mann's freedom. Mann himself had been a compliant prisoner – opening his diaries and other documents to investigators, accusing others of being part of the scheme and talking openly and in detail about the plot. The government in Malabo wanted British authorities to prosecute others, in return for Mann's freedom, but I doubt that Scotland Yard was in a position to do such a deal, even if (which is unlikely) political authorities thought getting Mann's release was a priority. Certainly the government in Equatorial Guinea didn't seek a big bribe to free Mann: as one of Africa's main producers of oil, the country is awash with cash.'

A week after Mann's release, *The Independent on Sunday* reported that he had been urged by Foreign Office officials to remain silent about the coup and to settle for a 'quiet life' with his wife and family. One close friend told the newspaper: 'The Foreign Office didn't do anything to help him get out of that place but they have been very quick to try to get him to play ball now that he is back. Simon has been told it would be in everyone's interests if he could just draw a line under this whole thing. We know the Foreign Office wants to get on side with EG (Equatorial Guinea) as quickly as possible but, frankly, it is also in their own interests for people to stop asking questions about this whole affair.

At the end of November, Man gave an interview to the BBC, reiterating South Africa's backing of his attempted coup, 'because if they are very good friends of the new government it would be of great benefit to South Africa because they know perfectly well that billions of dollars are at stake.'

Mann also strengthened his link with Mark Thatcher with the revelation that Margaret Thatcher stayed in the garden cottage at her son's home and that Mann 'always sat next to her at dinner parties. She liked me. We even went on holiday together.'

There was obviously acrimony between those involved in the plot – and repercussions. Thatcher, while saying Mann was still a friend of his, said he would give him a 'bloody good kicking'. Thatcher and Greg Wales severed all contact. Mann's long-suffering wife Amanda banned him from staying in touch with his co-conspirators. The film-maker James Brabazon said that the approach to him to cover the coup was to 'help press home to the outside world that this was a coup by African freedom fighters, justly overthrowing what is after all one of the world's most corrupt and murderous regimes.' But he added that the fifty or so soldiers recruited – and who claim they were never given the full picture of the attempted coup – now live in near destitution in South Africa, 'are unemployable, tainted with the charge of criminality and are bitterly angry at having never been compensated by Mann and the others. They feel they have been left to suffer the consequences.' One of those was Eduardo Tchmuichi whose daughter Cecilia said at the time of his arrest: 'Eduardo told us he was going off to do a job but he didn't tell us where. Later I saw on TV that some men had been arrested in Zimbabwe but it was only when we read a list of names in the newspaper we knew Eduardo was there. It was a terrible shock.'

Mann, himself, still felt the need for 'justice' for those he felt had abandoned him to his fate, left him to carry the can and who had not looked after his wife and children while he was ensconced in jail thousands of miles away.

As *The Independent on Sunday* reported: 'it is clear that, despite the bliss photographs with his wife Amanda, in the new Forest, Mann's return home is no neat ending to the sorry saga. For many individuals, organisations and foreign governments, it could initiate an uncomfortable fresh chapter as questions are asked about the circumstances behind the audacious attempt to depose a hardline ruler and take control of his nations' oil supplies.'

Exiled Equatorial Guinea president Severo Moto said he still found Mann 'charming'. Guardsman Nigel Morgan, under suspicion of revealing Mann's plans, said he saw no reason for any conflict between them and commented: 'I don't see huge problems. Simon has said he thinks the coup was a huge mistake and that's what we were telling him before he was arrested. So we can all agree on that now.' Nick du Toit settled back in South Africa and although he has not had any contact with Mann, says: 'I knew exactly what I was letting myself in for, so the fact that it all went wrong, I can't blame anybody.'

Not everyone still felt that way about Mann. One man who is still bitter is Viktor Dracula who says he still expects an apology – and payment of the £30,000 he was promised. 'We will watch to see how he conducts himself and hope that he contacts us to finalise this mess – but if he does not we will make him pay. The thought of Simon Mann getting rich on the back of what he did to us is sickening. He risked our lives, tricked us and then didn't even pay us like he promised. He was sending us to die like sardines and didn't even have the manners to tell us.'

Britain's Scotland Yard police force says their investigations into any British links with the plot are ongoing. But a senior Home Office source has claimed that although the Metropolitan Police visited Mann at least three times in prison and received relevant documents from the EG authorities, they were 'essentially going through the motions ... they are being asked to nail someone for perhaps planning an operation that in the end didn't take place. I don't see any will to ask any officer to push this too hard.'

There were those who were quick to point out the similarity between Mann's activities and the plot in author Frederick Forsyth's novel *The Dogs of War* (the book which had apparently fired the imagination of the coup plotters) though Mann's story had far more twists, turns and dubious characters. Forsyth's story tells how a British businessman hires mercenaries to overthrow the government of oil-rich Equatorial Guinea. It was all enough for one commentator, Canadian journalist Gwynne Dyer, based in London to state: 'Simon Mann belongs to that class of English ex-public schoolboys, expensively educated but too dim to work in the high end of business and finance that is the preferred career for their brighter contemporaries, who end up, perhaps after a stint in the army, living off their inherited money, their contacts and their presumptive status as respectable people.'

The website declarepeace.org.uk summed it up: 'It is a story with implausible characters and plot twists. There is the alleged cannibal dictator, his playboy son and scheming relatives. There is the offshore oil waiting to make millionaires out of those audacious or desperate enough to seize it. There is the exiled politician and the Chelsea plutocrat. There is the planeload of mercenaries stopping in Harare to pick up weapons. And, at the heart of it all, there is Simon Mann. How the plot went awry and landed this unusual Englishman in manacles may come to be judged as the end of an era of white buccaneers who thought they ruled Africa.'

In December 2009, Mann's audacious coup attempt was again told in a *Storyville* film for BBC Four. 'A failed coup attempt ... a British mercenary in a grim African prison ... a dictator accused by the West of torture ... and beneath it all, a spectacular underwater oil reserve that the world's major powers would love to get their hands on. It may sound like the latest John le Carre bestseller, but it's the real-life intrigue behind Simon Mann's African Coup, *Storyville*'s penetrating look at mysterious goings on in Equatorial Guinea, a tiny West African nation newly rich from oil and infamous for corruption. Filmed over eighteen months, with access to key players, the film offers a unique look inside a country that rarely allows in the foreign press ... This fast-paced thriller of a film travels the globe to unravel that plot, from South Africa to Spain, from London to Washington – promising to reveal the truth of what happened in the most controversial coup attempt in recent history.'

In February 2010, commentator Eric Leech wrote: 'Many questions remain, such as why did an experienced SAS soldier (Mann) allow himself to be so easily caught? Why were they trying to overthrow a nation's leader to take control of his oil supplies? Was it all about the wonga, or were there other forces at work? Unfortunately, it is these *other forces*, that will keep us from ever knowing the truth, but this story is far from over. With billions of dollars of oil on the line, a corrupt leader still in power, and the main players still on the hot seat, the fat lady is far from singing her last duet with Mann ...'

Chapter 12

Picking up the Pieces

In March 2010, Mann's 39-year-old wife gave an extraordinary account to *Tatler* magazine of his time in jail. She told how he dined on food not only of large proportions but prepared by a hotel chef. Mrs Mann said: 'The president arranged for hotel meals every day and Simon said he knew which chef was on that day by the food they cooked but he never ate all of it because he wanted to stay trim and slim.' Mann reportedly requested vegetables and salads, chicken to red meat and asked that no salt was added.

Amanda Mann said that when treated for his hernia problems he was cared for in the 'fabulous' president's private clinic and that all her fears about her 57-year-old husband being treated badly were unfounded. Her initial anxiety about having to tell the couple's four children that their father would not be coming home had been allayed.

'Little did I know that President Obiang was busy being a lovely, lovely man and giving me back the man I love and the father of my children. He was changing the way he ran his country and looking to reform, and his treatment of Simon was a sign of that. I never knew the president was going to be as fabulous as he was and I'm eternally grateful to him.' So grateful had she and her husband been that they had sent Obiang a book about the New Forest, close to their Hampshire home, as a 'thank you' present.

Mrs Mann also admitted she had been on the verge of leaving her husband when he was imprisoned because she had simply not known if she would see him again. She was less forthcoming about knowing anything about the attempted coup, saying: 'He wasn't like, "I'm off to buy a coat and then I'm off to do a coup." He was here and there . . . if I were a neurotic person, I would now be dead or at the bottom of a bottle of gin. You have to live and let live. And he could just as easily have been run over by a bus. I'm pretty laid back.'

Said a friend: 'None of us thought that at that age, fifty, with all his wealth and a family and with a wife with a bun in the oven he'd go on another bloody adventure.'

Added old friend and MP Henry Bellingham: 'If he had a fault, it was that he was an adventurer. And if the story of Equatorial Guinea is true, it was an adventure too far.'

It emerged that Obiang had called for two guarantees from Britain; that Mann's release was to be seen as the president's personal decision without any outside pressure, and that Mann and his family would never criticise Equatorial Guinea in relation to his treatment (or anyone else's) in prison or the sentencing.

In June 2010, Mann and his wife made a rare public appearance when they attended the launch party of a book on Princes William and Harry at Wheeler's restaurant in London's St James's.

In July 2010 it was reported that the Manns had sold their Hampshire home Inchmery to Lady Edwina Grosvenor, the 28-year-old daughter of the Duke of Westminster (Britain's richest land-owner) for £10m – some £4m more than its market value. Said a friend: 'They had no plans to sell but they were made an offer they couldn't refuse and realised it was an opportunity to turn the page. It wasn't marketed and it was one of those life-changing offers. During the years Simon was away, the house was incredibly important to Amanda because she could lock herself and the children away too. It is very private, with its own beach looking out to the Isle of Wight and the Solent and was perfect for someone who needed to stay out of the public eye. Amanda has no need for a fortress now.'

That same month, it was reported that the fortunes of one Tony Buckingham, one of Mann's former business partners in Executive Outcomes and Sandline International, somewhat overshadowed the financial ones of Mann – he was to pocket an £84.5m from the Heritage Oil gas and oil company of which he is chief executive. The windfall followed the sale of the company's fifty per cent stake in a series of oil exploration assets in Uganda.

In September 2010, Richard Kay in the *Daily Mail* reported that Mann would not be called to testify against Mark Thatcher or the

'Mr Big' businssman. Wrote Kay: 'I understand Mann has been "very co-operative" whenever police have talked to him about the plot, but according to well-placed sources, there was a reluctance to mount a case on what the old Etonian former SAS solider had alleged. Senior figures were said to be concerned at the can of worms such a case might open.' Mann was told his testimony would not be necessary and that the investigation was to be dropped.

That same month in *The Daily Dispatch* Mayibongwe Maqhina, Senior Political Correspondent, wrote how there was an investigation by PriceWaterhouseCoopers on behalf of the Eastern Cape Department of Health into health officials who had allegedly used a medical services aircraft for a private jaunt to Bloemfontein, South Africa to watch a football match. It said that the report suggested 'more widespread corruption could be exposed' through a criminal investigation by police.' There were disciplinary hearings against six of the eight implicated officials and Shnaks Maharah, former director of the emergency medical service had resigned. The man who paid for the officials' accommodation and match tickets was Aerocare's Crause Steyl who was subcontracted by National Airways Corporation – and of course, was the pilot who flew the Boeing 727 in the attempted coup with Mann. Steyl owned the aircraft and sub-leased it to the NAC.

So will Mann now take a backseat from trying to change the politics of foreign countries and lead a quiet life? It is hard to believe. Commented author Adam Roberts: 'It would be simplistic to see Mann as a proxy for western interests as a whole, but some will reckon that the only thing outsiders care about is getting control of Africa's natural resources. Mann may say he had more noble ambitions – that he had great pity for the ordinary people of Equatorial Guinea who were suffering repression – but his interests in fact seem largely personal. He wanted an adventure, the chance to act out a thriller with him as the hero. He also wanted that big "splodge of wonga". Perhaps he can get a job playing the lead role in *The Wonga Coup: The Movie.'*

There is talk of a movie of course – why the whole story cries out for one! And Mann is penning his own memoirs. How could he not?

But has Mann learned his lesson? By the very nature of their profession it is hard to keep a mercenary down and one cannot help but feel his name will hit the headlines again in the future.

Chapter 13

Round Up of the Coup That Never Was

December 2003/January 2004: Former South African special forces commander (and occasional adviser to Obiang) Johann Smith, hears rumours of the planned coup and sends two highly-detailed reports about it to two senior officers in British intelligence, to Michael Westphal, a senior colleague of Donald Rumsfeld, America's Secretary of Defence, and to South African Intelligence.

2004
7 March: A band of suspected mercenaries, including Simon Mann are arrested at Harare airport in Zimbabwe while others are rounded up elsewhere. Crause Steyl, waiting in Mali for word that the coup was a success before flying into Equatorial Guinea with exiled Severo Moto, escapes arrest. Severo Moto is immediately flown back to Madrid, Spain.

8 March: President of Equatorial Guinea, Teodoro Obiang Nguema, announces that fifteen mercenaries who planned to overthrow his regime were arrested in his country and said that exiled opposition leader Moto was behind the coup plot.

10 March: President Teodoro Obiang thanks South Africa and Angola for warning him of the plot and says it was funded by 'enemy powers' and multinational companies operating within Equatorial Guinea.

159

17 March: Those held in Zimbabwe are charged with conspiring to murder President Obiang.

31 March: Mann writes a letter pleading with associates, including Sir Mark Thatcher, to get him out of prison.

27 July: Sixty-seven of the seventy suspected mercenaries plead guilty to lesser charges of violating Zimbabwe's immigration and civil aviation laws.

28 July: Mann pleads guilty to attempting to possess dangerous weapons.

23 August: Fourteen mercenaries and five local men go on trial in Malabo, Equatorial Guinea, accused of being an advanced party for the mercenaries held in Zimbabwe.

25 August: Sir Mark Thatcher, the son of former UK Prime Minister Margaret Thatcher, is arrested at home by South African police in an early morning raid.

Thatcher is charged with violating South Africa's anti-mercenary law in connection with an alleged plot to topple the government of Equatorial Guinea.

He is later placed under house arrest and protests he is 'innocent of all charges' made against him.

27 August: It is reported that the government of Equatorial Guinea has asked for South Africa to extradite Thatcher. Zimbabwe acquits sixty-six of the suspected mercenaries of weapons charges.

28 August: Equatorial Guinea says it is seeking international arrest warrants for Thatcher and other Britons implicated in the alleged plot.

31 August: The court in Equatorial Guinea suspends proceedings on prosecutors' requests for more information about the alleged role Thatcher and others said to have financed the attempted coup.

During this month Jack Straw issues a strong denial that Britain had known anything about a planned coup.

1 September: Baroness Thatcher is reported to have posted the 2m rand ($334,000) bail for her son who remains under house arrest in Cape Town.

3 September: Thatcher is freed from house arrest after the bail bond is paid.

10 September: Mann is found guilty of weapons charges by a Zimbabwe magistrate and sentenced to seven years in prison. This was later reduced to four. In his absence, he was also found guilty in Equatorial Guinea in November that year, even though his 'trial' would not take place until later. The Harare court also hands out six month sentences to the two pilots of the plane that landed in Zimbabwe carrying the suspected mercenaries. The sixty-five men who were on the plane, convicted of immigration offences, are given twelve-month sentences.

14 November: Equatorial Guinea demands further explanation following UK Home Secretary Jack Straw's parliamentary answer that the UK government had known about the coup plot 'in late January 2004'.

16 November: Trial of South African Nick du Toit starts in Malabo.

18 November: Equatorial Guinea confirms it has charged Sir Mark in connection with the alleged coup plot.

Thatcher is accused of having helped finance the coup attempt, according to the country's Attorney General Jose Olo Obono.

24 November: The Cape Town High Court upholds a subpoena from the South African Justice Ministry that requires Thatcher to answer under oath questions from Equatorial Guinean authorities regarding the alleged coup attempt. (He was due to face questioning on 25 November 2004, regarding offences under the South African Foreign Military Assistance Act but the proceedings were later postponed until 8 April 2005.)

26 November: Nick du Toit and Equatorial Guinean opposition leader Severo Moto are found guilty of attempting to oust President Obiang.

Du Toit receives a thirty-four-year jail term and Mr Moto, who is in exile in Spain, is given sixty-three years in absentia.

2005
13 January: Thatcher appears in court in South Africa where he pleads guilty over his part in the alleged plot but denies he knew

exactly what was going on, claiming he financed a helicopter thinking it was to be used for humanitarian reasons. Thatcher agrees a plea-bargain to avoid jail and is given a suspended four-year sentence. He is also fined 3m rand ($500,000). Thatcher leaves South Africa.

Mann's lawyer says his client's sentence in Zimbabwe has been reduced from seven to four years on appeal.

15 May: Zimbabwe frees sixty-two South Africans more than a year after they were arrested, but South Africa says the next day it will charge them under its strict anti-mercenary laws.

19 September: Mark and Diane Thatcher announce their intention to divorce.

2006
30 June: BBC Two screens *Coup!* a satirical look at a 'tale of audacity, incompetence and betrayal' – Mann's thwarted coup attempt.

2007
9 May: Mann expects to be released early after his sentence is reduced but a Zimbabwean magistrate rules that he can be extradited to Equatorial Guinea. He appeals.

June: *The Mail on Sunday* newspaper is allowed access to Black Beach prison where Nick du Toit and other co-conspirators are incarcerated.

2008
30 January: Mann is deported to Equatorial Guinea from Zimbabwe to face coup plot charges after losing an appeal against extradition. He had served four years for buying weapons without a licence.

He is flown to Equatorial Guinea and taken to Black Beach prison. His lawyers insist he was illegally removed by being moved in secret before an appeal process was finished. The Foreign Office protests.

7 February: Eight MPs, headed by Lord Bingham of Cornhill, manage to stop the hearing into Mann's case because of Equatorial Guinea's refusal to guarantee his welfare and legal rights.

8 March: Britain's Channel 4 television station wins a legal battle to broadcast an interview with Mann during which he named British political figures including ministers and others involved in the coup attempt.

11 March: Mann says he plotted to oust Equatorial Guinea's president, but the scheme failed.

28 March: Equatorial Guinea issues an arrest warrant for Thatcher.

30 March: Guinea's public prosecutor says that Mann has testified that Thatcher knew all about the scheme to overthrow President Obiang.

18 June: Mann's trial starts. The day before *The Sunday Times* told how Equatorial Guinea was on 'high alert' for the proceedings. The prosecution asks that Mann be jailed for thirty-two years for his role in the coup plot. During the trial Mann says that Thatcher was part of the plot.

20 June: On the last day of his trial, Mann requests leniency, saying he was sorry for having been part of the plot.

7 July: Mann is sentenced to thirty-four years and four months in jail by an Equatorial Guinea court for his role in the plot.

That month the British-based businessman tells the *Daily Telegraph* he supported regime change in the oil-rich West African nation of Equatorial Guinea and financed plans by Moto to return to his country. He denies there had ever been a coup plot or that Thatcher was involved.

August: Former Conservative MP Rupert Allason, a military and intelligence expert, meets up with Equatorial Guinea's ambassador Nze Nfumu to continue negotiations to secure Mann's release from jail.

3 September: Severo Moto gives an exclusive interview to the *Daily Telegraph* in which he admits hiring Simon Mann for the Equatorial Guinea coup. He says the two men had met on several occasions in his exiled home of Madrid and that an agreement was struck for Mann to provide protection so he could return to Equatorial Guinea and 'fight for democratic change'.

2009

18 February: An armed group launches an attack on the presidential palace in Malabo, the capital of Equatorial Guinea. President Obiang was not in residence at the time. State media said the gunmen involved were from a Nigerian rebel group – and fifteen people were arrested in connection with the attack.

There was speculation that it might have been an attempt to rescue British mercenary Mann.

3 November: Equatorial Guinea's government pardons Mann, du Toit and three other South Africans on humanitarian grounds.

An adviser to the president, Miguel Mifuno, tells the BBC Mann has to leave the country within twenty-four hours.

2010

March: Mann's 39-year-old wife Amanda gives an account to *Tatler* magazine of his time in jail. She told how he dined on food not only of large proportions but prepared by a hotel chef.

July: It is reported that the Manns had sold their Hampshire home Inchmery to Lady Edwina Grosvenor, the 28-year-old daughter of the Duke of Westminster (Britain's richest landowner) for £10m – some £4m more than its market value.

Chapter 14

The Discovery and Damnation of Equatorial Guinea

1471: Portuguese navigator Fernao do Po sights the island of Fernando Po (now called Bioko).

1777: Portugal cedes islands of Annobon and Fernando Poo as well as rights on the mainland coast to Spain, giving it access to a source of slaves.

1844: Spanish settle in what became the province of Rio Muni – mainland Equatorial Guinea.

1904: Fernando Po and Rio Muni become the Western African Territories, later renamed Spanish Guinea.

1943: Severo Moto Nsa is born in Equatorial Guinea. He later becomes the most notable opposition politician in Equatorial Guinea, and leader of the Progress Party.

1968: After pressure from Equatorial Guinean nationalists and the United Nations, Spanish Guinea is granted independence and becomes the Republic of Equatorial Guinea with Francisco Macias Nguema as president who proclaims himself God's 'unique miracle.' He also drives the economy into the ground and over a third of the population goes into exile.

1968 August: A referendum is held In the presence of a UN observer team with the referendum and sixty-three per cent of the electorate voting in favour of the constitution which provides for a government with a General Assembly and a Supreme Court with judges appointed by the president.

1968–1969: President Francisco Macias Nguema murders a sixth of the population of Equatorial Guinea.

1972: Nguema becomes president for life.

1974: Formal education in Equatorial Guinea comes to an end.

1979: Nguema ousted in military coup led by his nephew Teodoro Obiang Nguema Mbasogo and is executed.

1991: Alba, Equatorial Guinea's third significant oil field, twelve miles north of Bioko island is discovered by Water International. Original estimates of reserves at Alba are around sixty-eight million barrels of oil equivalent (BOE), but recent exploration has increased new estimates to almost 1 billion BOE.

1992: Qualitative restrictions on imports, non-tariff protection, and many import licensing requirements are lifted when the government adopts a public investment program endorsed by the World Bank.

1993: First multi-party elections are condemned as fraudulent and are boycotted by the opposition.
The World Bank severs its relationship with Equatorial Guinea.

1995: Equatorial Guinea's Zafiro field, located northwest of Bioko island, is discovered by ExxonMobil and Ocean Energy (bought by Devon Energy in 2003). It contains the majority of the country's oil reserves.

1996 February: President Obiang Nguema wins ninety-nine per cent of votes in election amid reports of widespread irregularities. Worldwide, critics say the campaign was marred by fraud (most of the opposition candidates had withdrawn in the final week). In an attempt to appease his critics, Obiang gives minor portfolios in his cabinet to people identified as opposition figures.

1996 March: Mobil oil corporation announces it has discovered sizeable new oil and gas reserves.

1997: The government initiates efforts to attract significant private sector involvement through cooperative efforts with a visit from the Corporate Council on Africa and numerous ministerial efforts.

1998: The government privatizes distribution of petroleum products. There are now Total and Mobil stations in the country

1998 January: Amnesty International reports the arrest of scores of people, mostly from the Bubi minority, following attacks on military posts on Bioko island.

1998 June: A military tribunal sentences fifteen people to death for separatist attacks on Bioko island.

1999: The Equatorial Guinea government budget is $47m.
  Ceiba, Equatorial Guinea's second major producing oil field, off Rio Muni is discovered by Amerada Hess and is estimated to contain 300–800m barrels of oil

1999 March: Ruling Democratic Party of Equatorial Guinea wins the majority of seats in parliamentary elections – which are again condemned as fraudulent. Dozens of members of main opposition Popular Union are arrested. The main opposition parties refuse the seats they had allegedly won.

2000: The maritime border with Nigeria is settled, allowing Equatorial Guinea to continue exploitation of its oil fields.

2000 May: Obiang's ruling PDGE again overwhelms its rivals in local elections.

2001: Oil revenue in Equatorial Guinea reaches $140m. Equatorial Guinea's economy emerges as one of world's fastest-growing because of oil exploitation. Opposition says trickle-down effect of growth is too slow and too small.
  GEPetrol is established as Equatorial Guinea's national oil company. It was originally to be the primary state-run institution responsible for the country's downstream oil sector activities. However, since 2001 its primary focus has become the management of the government's stakes in various Production Sharing Contracts (PSCs) with foreign oil companies. GEPetrol also partners with foreign firms to undertake exploration projects and has a say in the

country's environmental policy implementation. In its recent block-licensing negotiations, Equatorial Guinea has pursued increases in the government's stake in new PSCs.

2001 March: Eight exiled opposition parties form a coalition in Spain to overhaul politics at home, saying democracy under Obiang is a sham.

2001 July: Exiled politician Florentino Ecomo Nsogo, head of the Party of Reconstruction and Social Well-Being (PRBS), returns home as the first opposition figure to respond to an appeal by President Obiang Nguema, who wants opposition parties to register.

2002: The African Development Bank and the European Union co-finance two projects to improve the paved roads from Malabo to Luba and Riaba; and to build an interstate road network to link Equatorial Guinea to Cameroon and Gabon. A Chinese construction company is completing a project to link Mongomo to Bata on the mainland

2002 April: The World Bank resumes lending to Equatorial Guinea.

2002 June: A court jails sixty-eight people for up to twenty years for an alleged coup plot against President Obiang Nguema. They include main opposition leader Placido Mico Abogo. The EU is concerned that confessions were obtained under duress. Amnesty International says many defendants showed signs of torture. There were numerous irregularities associated with the trial, including evidence of torture and a lack of substantive proof.

2002 December: President Obiang Nguema is re-elected. Authorities say he won 100 per cent of the vote. Opposition leaders had pulled out of the poll, citing fraud and irregularities. Following his re-election Obiang forms a government based on national unity encompassing all opposition parties, except for the CPDS, which declined to join after Obiang refused to release one of their jailed members.

2003 August: Exiled opposition leaders form self-proclaimed government-in-exile in Madrid, Spain.
   Opposition leader Placido Mico Abogo and seventeen other political prisoners released.

2003 October: Washington reopens its embassy on the island capital of Malabo after an eight-year shutdown. Obiang has had his opponents imprisoned and tortured, his presidential predecessor executed by firing squad, and has helped himself to the state treasury at will.

2003 November: The government announces an ambitious ten-project program to upgrade the country's road network and improve the airport facilities at Bata, the country's second city. (These projects have since been completed and additional airport expansion and new-city corridors are now under construction.)

2004 March: Zimbabwean police in Harare impound a plane from South Africa with sixty-four mercenaries on board. The group said they were providing security for a mine in Democratic Republic of the Congo, but a couple of days later an Equatorial Guinean minister said they had detained fifteen more men who he claimed were the advance party for the group captured in Zimbabwe. Nick du Toit, the leader of the group of South Africans, Armenians, and one German in Equatorial Guinea, said at his trial in Equatorial Guinea that he was playing a limited role in a coup bid organized by Simon Mann, the leader of the group held in Zimbabwe, to remove Obiang from power and install an exiled opposition politician, Severo Moto. Suspected mercenaries are detained in Zimbabwe. A crackdown on immigrants ensues and hundreds of foreigners are deported.

2004 April: Parliamentary and municipal elections take place. President Obiang's Democratic Party of Equatorial Guinea (PDGE) and allied parties win 98 of 100 seats in parliament and all but seven of 244 municipal posts. International observers criticized both the election and its results.

2004 June: Obiang reorganizes the cabinet and creates two new positions – Minister of National Security and Director of National Forces. The prime minister is appointed by the president and operates under powers designated by the president.

2004 July: All but three of seventy suspected mercenaries accused of plotting a coup in Equatorial Guinea plead guilty to lesser charges in Zimbabwe.

169

Equatorial Guinea and Gabon reach an agreement allowing joint oil exploration in disputed territories following a final resolution worked out under UN mediation. They have disputed the ownership of three islands in the Gulf of Guinea, including Mbagne Island, since the 1970s.

2004 August: Mark Thatcher is arrested and charged with helping to finance the foiled coup attempt in oil rich Equatorial Guinea.

2004 September: Simon Mann is sentenced to seven years in jail in Zimbabwe after being convicted of illegally trying to buy weapons. In subsequent legal proceedings, three Equatoguineans and three South Africans are acquitted.

2004 October: The government caps oil production at 350,000 barrels per day to extend the life of the country's petroleum reserves. It lifted the cap the next year to allow expansion.

2005 January: Thatcher pleads guilty to unwittingly helping to finance the foiled coup and receives a $506,000 fine and suspended jail sentence.

Equatorial Guinea pledges to increase transparency in its fiscal accounts, citing its new natural gas company as a first step in this direction.

2005 March: A US Senate investigators releases a new report that says nine American banks, including Citigroup, Bank of America, and Riggs Bank, enabled Augusto Pinochet, former Chilean dictator, and family members to build a secret network of accounts to conceal his wealth. DC-based Riggs Bank merges with PNC Financial following the inquiry, which also reveals that Pinochet and Obiang Nguema, president of Equatorial Guinea, had stashed millions in private accounts there.

It is reported that China's influence in Africa is expanding rapidly. Chinese projects include the rebuilding of Nigeria's railroad network; the paving of roads in Rwanda; ownership of copper mines in Zambia; timber operations in Equatorial Guinea; and supermarket operations in Lesotho.

2005 June: President Obiang grants amnesty to the six Armenian pilots involved in the 2004 attempted coup.

2006 October: Japanese Prime Minister Shinzo Abe says his country will continue assisting Equatorial Guinea in its efforts to promote democracy. Abe makes the pledge during a 45-minute meeting with Equatorial Guinea's President Teodoro Obiang Nguema in Tokyo.

2007: The government undertakes a $336m Social Development Fund project, which engages US Agency for International Development (USAID) to improve the quality of life and raise standards in education and health care.

2007 January: China's foreign minister continues his whistle-stop African tour in Equatorial Guinea, where he cancels debt, promises aid and opens a new Chinese-built media centre.

2007 February: Equatorial Guinea is cited as the world's third richest country with a GDP per person estimated at $50,000.

2007 April: Equatorial Guinea is one of six central African countries which plan to launch a common passport permitting the free movement of goods and people across their borders.

2007 May: A Zimbabwean court authorises the extradition of Simon Mann to Equatorial Guinea sweeping aside concerns that he might face torture or invalid justice there.

2008: The government revenue is around $7,056 billion. Oil revenues account for more than eighty-one per cent of government revenue. Value added tax and trade taxes are other large revenue sources for the government. The government announces a $2.2 billion purchase of US-based Devon Energy's stake in the country's oil fields, increasing its participation to twenty per cent in the Zafiro field operation.

Equatorial Guinea is ranked by Transparency International as the world's ninth most corrupt country. Obiang spends less than two per cent of the GDP on public health and less than one per cent on education.

2008 May: Legislative elections result in an overwhelming victory for Obiang's PDGE. Ninety-nine of the 100 seats in the assembly go to the PDGE while the opposition party, the Convergence for Social Democracy (CPDS), only receive one. (This is one less seat than the 2004 elections that granted the CPDS two seats.) Results were similar in the municipal elections held the same day, granting the PDGE 319 councilor seats while CPDS only gained 13. International elections observers report that the elections were generally conducted in a free and fair manner. Nevertheless, irregularities are reported. These include the barring of certain members of the international press.

2008 June: During Mann's trial he reportedly confesses to the 2004 attempted coup, implicating Severo Moto, Sir Mark Thatcher and a nationalised British citizen with connections to Nigeria.

Obiang grants amnesty to thirty-seven political prisoners and the government indicates a willingness to grant amnesty to other political prisoners. The country is undertaking an ambitious, multi-billion dollar development program that is 'improving the quality of life and providing opportunities for employment for its citizens.' Equatorial Guinea is also a candidate in the Extractive Industries Transparency Initiative (EITI), which aims to 'clean up' the accountability in the oil, gas and minerals sector.

2008 July: Mann is sentenced to thirty-four years in prison but allowed visits by western media and family members.

2008 August: Equatorial Guinea's exiled opposition leader Severo Moto is released from a Spanish jail four months after he was detained for allegedly trying to send weapons to the oil-rich African nation.

2009: Exports to the US total and consist overwhelmingly of petroleum products. US exports to Equatorial Guinea total $304m and consist mainly of machinery, articles of iron or steel, measuring instruments, and chemical products.

China starts drilling in a new offshore block.

2009 January: In Libreville, Gabon, leaders of the six Central African states (Cameroon, Chad, Gabon, CAR, Congo, Equatorial Guinea), begin meeting to discuss closer economic ties, including the creation of a new regional airline. The Economic and Monetary Union of Central Africa, known as CEMAC, plan discussions on such issues as monetary reform and the free movement of citizens.

2009 February: Gunmen in boats attack the Presidential Palace in Malabo. Equatorial Guinean security forces successfully repel

172

the dawn raiders. Obiang was on the mainland in Bata during the unsuccessful attack. The government accuses the Nigerian rebel group, Movement for the Emancipation of the Niger Delta (MEND), of carrying out the attack.

2009 May: Obiang, together with Gabon's Omar Bongo and the Republic of Congo's Denis Sassou Nguesso are investigated by a French judge over money laundering and other alleged crimes linked to their wealth in France. The probe follows a complaint by Transparency International France, an association that tracks corruption.

2009 November: Mann is pardoned and returns to the United Kingdom.

2009 December: The contract between the Government of Equatorial Guinea and USAID is renewed for an additional year.

2010 January: *New Zimbabwe* reports that continental hospitality and leisure group African Sun has shelved plans to venture into Equatorial Guinea due to the country's political instability.

2010 April: An Equatorial Guinea court sentences seven Nigerians to twelve years in prison on terrorism charges for their role in the February 2009 attack on the presidential palace – the attack officials denied at the time was an attempted coup. Two of the men were later reported to have died in detention.

2010 July: Under the headline 'Now "cannibal" dictator who set Simon Mann free bids to join Commonwealth', *The Mail on Sunday* reports that Obiang is seeking admission to the Commonwealth.

2010 August: Equatorial Guinea defends the execution of four former government officials convicted of attempting to assassinate Obiang during the attack on the presidential palace in February 2009. The four – JoseéAbeso Nsue, a former captain of the country's land forces, his deputy Manuel Ndong Anseme, member of the presidential security team Alipio Ndong Asumu and former customs chief Jacinto Michó Obiang – are executed immediately after being convicted by a military court in Malabo of being 'criminally responsible and the authors of an attack on the head of state and representative of the government, terrorism and treason.' The executions focussed the world's eyes once again on Equatorial Guinea.

2010 September: It is reported that Filiberto Ntutumu, Equatorial Guinea's Minister of Education, Science and Sport, had met with teachers and 'education professionals' to discuss future plans for improving the country's education system.

2010 October: World Habitat Day – held on the first Monday of October every year – in 2010 again brings focus on Equatorial Guinea when Amnesty International calls for an end to forced evictions in the country. Around 1,000 families since 2003 have been forcibly evicted from their homes to make room for roads, up-market housing, hotels and shopping centres.

Acknowledgements

Wisden
The Times
globalsecurity.org
Michael Gove, *The Times*
Hansard
Adam Roberts
The *Observer*
James Brabazon
Raymond Whitaker and Paul Lashmar, the *Observer*
First Post
The *Independent*
Tribune
Amnesty International
BBC Two
The Mail on Sunday
Channel 4T
The Independent on Sunday
World Socialist Web site, Ann Talbot
The Daily Telegraph
The Sunday Times
Will Ross, BBC West Africa correspondent
Head Heritage
Sue Turton, *Channel 4 News* correspondent
Frank Gardner, BBC security correspondent
Eric Leech
Tatler
Richard Kay, *Daily Mail*
Professor André Thomashausen, Unisa's Centre for International Law
Anthony Nota, *Legal Business*
Robert Young Pelton
Howard Teicher
Mark Hollingsworth, co-author of *Thatcher's Fortunes: The Life and Times of Mark Thatcher*
Harper's
Duncan Campbell
Afrol News
Nation
Patrick Smith, editor *Africa Confidential* magazine
Human Rights Watch
New Zimbabwe
Sharon Church, *The Mail on Sunday*
The Daily Dispatch
Vicky Ward, *Vanity Fair*
Natalie Clarke, *Daily Mail*

Index

178